DEATH ORG CHART

by Jeffrey DeMure, AIA

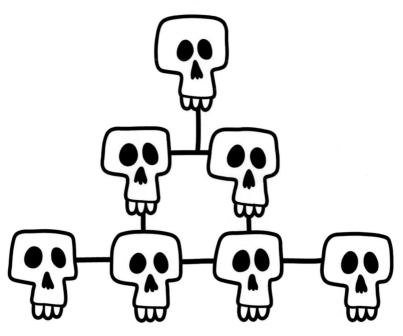

Fountainhead Publishing

Death to the Org Chart
Published by Fountainhead Publishing
Copyright © 2021 by Jeffrey DeMure, AIA
All rights reserved.

Fountainhead Publishing
5905 Granite Lake Drive, Suite 140
Granite Bay, California 95746
Email: fountainheadpublishing@jdaarch.com

Publishing and editorial team: Michael Levin Writing Company
www.michaellevinwrites.com
Project Manager and Editorial Director: Bryan Gage
Editor: Chelsea Richardson
Publishing Manager: Sara Stratton
Cover Design: Hugh MacLeod, Gapingvoid

Library of Congress Number: 2020924587
- ISBN: 978-1-7322070-3-5 – paperback
- ISBN: 978-1-7322070-4-2 – ebook

Ordering Information:
Quantity sales. Special discounts are available on quantity purchases by corporations, associations, and others. For details, contact the publisher at the address above.

Printed in United States of America.

6/1/21

DEAR JIM —

YOU ARE AN INSPIRATION...
KEEP PRESSING IN ...
KEEP PRESSING ON!

DEDICATION

For my wife, Melanie. When things are at their toughest, you and I are at our best, and whenever the bullets are flying, I can always count on you more than anyone else I've ever been able to in my entire life.

That's what ignites my passion for continuing to do more in life than should be possible—by punching way above my weight—because I'm married to a fearless competitor who fights for all the right things and never backs down.

When you have two people who are aligned on goals and united in love, anything is possible. And you are I are living proof of that. You are the love of my life.

CONTENTS

ACKNOWLEDGMENTS

The commitment to develop and idea—a principle—from start to finish is not something I do well without the encouragement and dedication from Chelsea Richardson. Your organizational, logistical, and relational gifts, and your understanding of how I work best has made this book possible. You always make things better!

This being my second book, and having a frame of reference for what it's worth to work with a writer, has given me a unique perspective to be able to compliment Bryan Gage from a vantage point of experience. You are a skillful extrapolator and miner for what is relevant, salient, and meaningful. Thank you!

As an architect and designer, 'if it doesn't look good, then don't bother' is my point of departure for most things in life. Overlay this with a colorful character and rapier wit, combined with an artistic style than blends with his heart and is always infused with positive, loving consideration, and you get Hugh MacLeod. You are a tremendous inspiration, and I'm grateful for the work you've done on these pages.

A principle is only as good as the people who are willing to embrace it, and the proving grounds for the Q^3 Quad Mod was the dynamic team at Jeffrey DeMure + Associates. Always positive, always appropriately skeptical, always willing to embrace a good idea when it honors the individuals and feeds the culture. Thank you all for helping me to create this incredible extended family.

It's only possible to be successful in life at a high level when you can see what's possible. The Strategic Coach program has the ability to unlock that within entrepreneurs who are willing to invest in themselves through the program and reach a much higher level, not just in business, but in life. Thank you to Dan and Babs and the whole Strategic Coach team, and to my coach, Adrienne Duffy. Your ability to unlock the potential of the entrepreneurs you work with is remarkable.

To my four amazing children who teach me way more than I teach them. It's the toughest consulting gig that I've ever had. Thank you for never compromising in your expectations of what a daddy should be.

FOREWORD

BY DAN SULLIVAN, FOUNDER AND PRESIDENT OF STRATEGIC COACH®

In coaching him as a longtime participant in the Strategic Coach® Program, it's been my pleasure to know Jeffrey DeMure and guide his progress as he has built an outstanding architectural firm.

One of the most important things Jeff has learned in Strategic Coach, and from meeting so many businesspeople in his work, is that it's all too easy for businesses to become stuck, unable to grow.

People go to business school and learn about how businesses should be organized. Instead of this information proving useful or helpful, it traps businesses, crippling their ability to grow and thrive.

Especially in these times where the business world is recovering from the effects of the COVID-19 pandemic, it's become more important than ever for businesses to move away from the backward-looking ideas that have kept them from achieving meaningful growth.

Death to the Org Chart is more than a book. It's a movement. It's a call for businesses to transform themselves from the old-school thinking that keeps their growth sharply limited.

It's a way of getting unstuck.

It's an opportunity for businesses to reimagine themselves—the way they organize themselves, the way they look at their various component parts, and the way they serve.

I believe that with this book, Jeff is going to transform the way businesses think and act.

Jeff isn't just offering a quick fix or a flavor-of-the-month approach to reorganizing, something that the team will nod their heads with in fake agreement while waiting for the whole thing to pass.

Instead, Jeff is showing all of us how businesses could and should be run. I believe that the methodology he teaches will transform not just the businesses who follow his guidance, but all businesses. Indeed, there will really only be two kinds of businesses going forward—those that abandon the traditional org chart in favor of collaboration, as Jeff insists, and those that get left behind or swept away.

I urge you not just to read this book but to put everything Jeff says into action. The result will be a happier team, where all of the functions of the business, both Back Stage and Front Stage, are respected and carried out to the fullest, but also a business that is growing, increasingly profitable, and best of all, fun to own.

Death to the Org Chart represents new life for all businesses . . . starting with yours.

Dan Sullivan
Toronto, Canada
September 2020

HOW I MET HUGH

I met Hugh MacLeod in 2013 when he spoke at The Vine conference in San Diego, California, and have been an admirer ever since. With his unassuming manner, Rapidograph pens, and Scottish brogue, Hugh is an enigma wrapped in an anomaly shrouded in mystery. Bright and early after a night of revelry, I spotted him in the corner of the conference with his digital sketchpad and wondered, 'Huh. I wonder how this is going to go?' Much to my surprise, at the conclusion of the program Hugh took the stage and proceeded to share his musings and sketches for each of the day's presentations, concisely summarizing the essence and feeling of each topic. Mic drop.

On a whim, I sent a note to Hugh asking if he'd be willing to illustrate my first book, *Livable Design*. To my great delight, he accepted that assignment along with the one you now hold in your hands. Hugh read the book and encapsulated each chapter in a piece of art and I couldn't be happier with the collaboration. Each chapter begins with one of his pieces accompanied by his musings on the subject.

Should you find yourself struggling for how to best convey your message, your voice or your culture, reach out to Hugh at @gapingvoid and experience the magic for yourself.

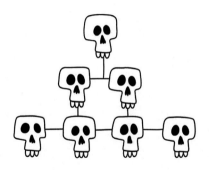

PROLOGUE

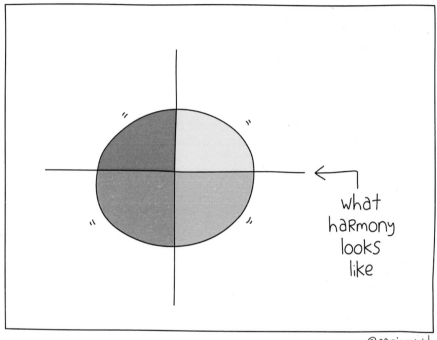

what
haRmony
looks
like

@gapingvoid

THIS IS OUR KEY TO HARMONY, THE Q³ QUAD MOD. The Front Stage (value creation), the Back Stage (confidence building), and the four quadrants that lie within: Marketing, Design, Production, and Operations. This is the whole crux of the book.

- Hugh MacLeod

PROLOGUE

Portland, Oregon, is cold and dreary in the middle of winter, and this winter day in 2010 was no exception. PDX, aka Portland International Airport, was particularly gray this day, but not terribly busy.

The inside of my head, however, was very busy! I was sitting by a ticket counter with Chelsea Richardson, my friend and colleague and a fellow principal at our architecture firm. We had just finished a long, difficult meeting with a client, and now we were waiting for our flight home. Chelsea was on the phone with a project manager from our office, and I was still mentally rehashing the conversation we'd had with the client less than an hour ago, and contemplating the decisions we'd made.

I was interrupted midthought by the phone ringing in my pocket. It was a call from our financial director, who was upset because our collection cycle had drifted to ninety-two days, which put us in a short-term cash crunch.

"How did we get so far down this road without me knowing about it?" I demanded.

"Well, I told you about it when you were leaving for your last trip," he replied.

I could swear it felt like my head literally exploded, just like in that infamous scene from David Cronenberg's 1981 cult classic, *Scanners*. I barely remembered the conversation he was talking about. "A comment and a nod is not a discussion!" I snapped at him. "And a discussion—particularly a brief, unfocused one—is *not* a decision!"

I hung up, frustrated and disappointed. Have you ever been there?

After a few deep breaths and a reassuring and knowing look from Chelsea, I was ready to assign blame where it rightfully belonged—on the maniac founder, CEO, and principal of our firm!

Yeah, that'd be me. As the cartoon character Pogo famously quipped, "We have met the enemy and he is us." Here we were in the midst of the Great Recession, trying to catch a falling knife without severing a critical artery, and my confidence was rattled. I'd been guilty of what I call "drive-by decision making." Sure, my financial director was largely at fault—collections were *his* responsibility, and he'd dropped the ball—but that didn't let me off the hook. Our business, for me, had become a mash-up of the public-facing side, the back room, and all the stuff in the middle, all of it leaching into this amorphous puddle of business, financial, and client goo. There were no distinctions among the various parts and pieces of the business, and each one was just as crucial as the next. We were governed by what Charles Hummel calls "the tyranny of the urgent," always doing what was acutely critical instead of what was important. It had become MBC—Management by Crisis—and whatever mistakes my financial director had made, the final responsibility lay with me.

Or was it his fault, after all? I would get these calls at the least opportune times, often not right *after* we'd had a tough meeting (as was the case today), but immediately *before*. It's difficult enough to have a substantive, value-oriented interaction with a client without having just gotten off a phone call in which you've realized that you and one of the directors of your organization are not on the same page. I wanted to call him right back and vent at him some more: "Why are you in a position of such responsibility if you don't understand the concept of time and place? When I need to go out there and get somebody excited about our work, that's not the time to tell me we're going to dip into our line of credit because you've been screwing up collections." Did he have no respect for the work I needed to do? Did he even understand what I did?

Of course, the fault was both his *and* mine. This was a result of the two of us not being on the same page in terms of when and how we communicated. I tended to make myself available to everyone in my organization at all times, as well as to clients and consultants; as a result, the lines blurred between the issues I'd be dealing with from one moment to the next.

In my frustration, I had sarcastically asked myself whether this guy even understood the work I did . . . but now I had to ask myself a similar question: Did *I* fully understand my own role in the company? Did I know where my purview began and ended? And to be fair, how deeply did I understand *his* job?

I realized then that there was a real problem with the way my organization was structured: no one had any awareness of where other people were working and what their objectives were when they were there. That's why this crisis had taken on such dramatic importance: I had been in a working-with-the-client mindset, and I was abruptly forced to deal with something that was very much a backroom situation. I suddenly realized it was unrealistic to switch gears that quickly and still be effective. I'd had enough, and I did not want to deal with it anymore.

Now to be clear, my frustration was mostly internal. The dedication, professionalism, and effectiveness of our team weren't concerns. The team wasn't the problem—indeed, it was only by dint of their talents that we'd survived our dysfunctional organizational structure for as long as we had.

But I knew I could do better—*be* better. I knew that my organization and I could become more effective, and that in the process we could make our work more enjoyable.

OK, I thought, this is going to require some serious focus. What's the first thing an inveterate visual thinker—who happens to be an architect—does at a time like this? He starts to sketch out the problem, to clarify the relationships between the seemingly unrelated elements that go into leading and running a professional design business.

And so, right there in the small seating area beside a PDX ticket counter, the Q^3 Quad Mod was born.

CHAPTER 1

YOU CAN'T HAVE ENTREPRENEURIAL
FREEDOM WITH YESTERDAY'S ORG CHART

@gapingvoid

WHY DO PEOPLE BECOME ENTREPRENEURS? A big reason is the freedom it affords them, being their own boss and whatnot. But that freedom isn't free, it comes at a price. That price can be extremely long hours, greater financial insecurity (certainly in the early days, but even after that) and the unrelenting stress of making a high-risk career move. Everyone's results will vary, be careful what you wish for.

- Hugh MacLeod

FREEDOM IS WAITING

Within all leaders there's a spirit of excellence just waiting to burst forth. This book is for anyone who is ready to set that spirit loose—that is, anyone who possesses an entrepreneurial spirit.

It's for those who have always had a desire to accomplish more than they could do by working for someone else, but have become frustrated in their attempts to reach the next level of success. They've tried doing things the way they think things *should* be done—the way the business community has told them they need to do things, because everybody does it this way, because "that's how it's done"—and found that these processes and methods are not producing the results they want.

Maybe you're a nine-to-five wage-earner dreaming of starting your own business. Or maybe you're already running a single-person, nonemployee business (like twenty-four million other American businesses[1]), and you aspire to build a larger company that earns enough revenue to employ a staff.

Or maybe you're what we call a *lone-wolf entrepreneur*— someone like an attorney or a dentist: you have five to ten employees, but the business can't run itself without you, and your personal relationships and mental health are suffering because you're overworked.

Or maybe you run a larger company with dozens of subordinates spread out beneath you in a pyramid-shaped organizational (org) chart, but you're finding that no matter how much you grow, you can't seem to achieve the kind of profitability you need—and like the lone wolf, you find your personal relationships and mental health are suffering because you're overworked, stressed out, and stretched thin.

However you define success, your dreams *are* attainable. What's missing in your professional life is entrepreneurial freedom—and I'm going to show you how to create that freedom for yourself.

WHY DO WE DO IT?

Why did you become an entrepreneur? Do you remember?

Thoreau said, "The mass of men lead lives of quiet desperation," and I think that's especially true in the business and professional design services worlds. Entrepreneurs, generally speaking, are people who feel a nameless, indefinable angst when they contemplate what it would be like to spend their lives punching a clock, their time at someone else's disposal.

Author and cofounder of Strategic Coach Dan Sullivan says the four freedoms of an entrepreneur are time, money, relationships, and purpose.[2] In all likelihood, you picked up this book because one or more of those freedoms is unduly constrained for you. The greatest freedom you can have is knowing that there is freedom to be had.

I remember vividly why I chose entrepreneurship. More than anything else, I wanted the freedom to control my own destiny. I didn't want to have to accept someone else's constraints on my time and creative energy. I didn't want anyone telling me what I should be doing from one moment to the next. And I didn't want anyone else to be able to define my success.

I used to have what most people consider a "regular job." I worked for a couple of architecture firms during that phase of my career, and I was very well taken care of. I had latitude and influence and perks and benefits . . . and I was restless. People who call themselves entrepreneurs will be able to relate to the feeling: "I don't want to do this anymore. I *can't* do this anymore. I'm miserable."

There's a verse in the Bible that I like very much: "Hope deferred makes the heart sick, but desire fulfilled is a tree of life." (Proverbs 13:12) If you've got a dream in your heart and you're not working toward it, then you're dying. That's what freedom means to an entrepreneur. It's about releasing yourself from the trap of a gilded cage. It's about being honest with yourself: "Yeah, I'm doing OK . . . but I'm miserable. I have a dream in my heart, and this is not it."

Entrepreneurship is freedom from the traditional paycheck model. That's the first freedom you need before you can achieve Sullivan's four freedoms—the freedom to have enough faith in yourself to believe that you can generate an income that will support you and your family. And to achieve this freedom, you need to believe you can build value in the process, that you can make others' lives better as a result of what you're doing.

Entrepreneurs live their lives very, very differently. It takes courage to accept the idea that if you don't sell something this quarter, this month, this week, then you're not going to eat.

THE TRAGEDY OF MISDIRECTED EFFORT

A lot of people spend an inordinate amount of time on activities that produce very limited results because they don't understand the basic premise under which they should be managing or leading. This has to do with what people *think* they should be doing versus what they *actually* should be doing.

I come from a small industrial/agrarian community in upstate New York, in the Hudson Valley, at the eastern end of the rust belt. There were factories in the larger towns and farms in the smaller towns. There was some affluence, but it wasn't in my neighborhood. This region, along with New England, is fertile ground for the Puritan work ethic—the notion that hard work, and hard work *alone*, allows you to be successful.

Today, that Puritan ethic remains alive and well in business. People believe they just need to knuckle down, put their noses to the grindstone, and they'll achieve success. That model is broken in the US, but people still live that way, it is still infused into the curricula of business and architecture schools, and it's rampant in industry in general.

Hard work is admirable, to be sure, but it's not the only driver of success, and by itself it's not enough. In these pages we'll explore small shifts you can make in your worldview, in your mindset, and in how you treat relationships, to maximize your enjoyment of your vocation. As a result, the people around you will be more effective because they'll understand what they're supposed to be doing, and they'll see better results from all that hard work.

I'm a commercial pilot. I own and operate three airplanes, so I fly a lot. If you're a sailor or a pilot, you understand that if you're just a couple of degrees off course, you're going to miss your mark—in fact, you won't get anywhere near it. The longer you wait, the further you will stray from it unless you make appropriate corrections. All the familiar landmarks go by, but they're just a little bit further away than they should be . . . and then a little bit *further* away, and next thing you know, you're lost.

This book, in part, is about course correction. It will remove the clouds that obscure your vision of the landmarks you need to navigate. And once you see the mountain after the clouds part, you can never not see the mountain again.

YESTERDAY'S ORG CHART

To stick with my piloting metaphor: If that mountain is your goal of entrepreneurial freedom, what's the most significant cause of the fog obscuring your vision of it?

It's the corporate org chart.

These charts were originally devised as a way to bring order to a business model that had very different goals than today's businesses do. The first organizational chart dates back to 1855, credited to Daniel McCallum and George Holt Henshaw of the New York and Erie Railroad. Their intent was to depict the flow of power, chain of command, and class of worker within the company. Does it work that way for some businesses? Maybe. But does it really *work*—that is, does it function to identify the path of responsibility to get to the people you need to reach and the teams that work together on projects to achieve shared results? If you've ever worked for a company that's held captive by one of these monstrosities, I'm sure you know the answer to that question.

Is the traditional org chart still relevant? Was it ever? Sure, in the middle of the nineteenth century, when real manufacturing was beginning and people commuted by horse and buggy! Today, we can adopt a better, simpler, more meaningful way to structure our businesses. The org chart is still widely seen as a requirement for the structure of a business, and so the board of directors, the lenders, the shareholders, and other stakeholders all want to see it. But do you think they have ever stopped to ask themselves why?

It's one of those things that people look at once and then throw away. They don't need the chart itself; they just want to know it exists.

I say, "Death to the org chart," because nobody really *uses* it.

Business depends on teamwork; it requires that everything be done through collaboration, and an organizational chart doesn't help you with that at all. It doesn't tell you whom you can collaborate with, or how that can happen. I'm a visual person—the kind of person who finds charts and diagrams appealing—and to my eye, if you look at an organizational chart, it doesn't speak to collaboration. Rather, it suggests a series of islands, each of which represents a work unit of sorts, and their relationship to other groups is a tenuous line.

Because the term *org chart* has been part of the business lexicon for half a century, people feel stupid if they ask a question about it. But it doesn't make sense to keep doing things the way they've always been done just because they've always been done this way. Indeed, at a time like this, when a global pandemic has upended everything we thought we knew about conducting business, it's especially important to be open to new ways of doing things—i.e., to be adaptable.

The idea that our work units should be set up according to an organizational chart that's deficient in the ways I've described above is crazy. Collaboration is an organic process, and regardless of what a company's org chart says, most people's real jobs—the work they actually do—overlap in a kind of three-dimensional Venn diagram.

In short, the org chart is a requirement in most businesses . . . and then it never gets used.

So what fills in the blank? Chaos. Where there's no structure, people are left to do things on their own, and you have *silos*. These little departments become fiefdoms within organizations, and everyone in the silo is incentivized to make their silo bigger and more influential, because then you get more people for your fiefdom . . . which gives you more influence within the organization.

These silos have impermeable walls, so the collective wisdom within them is never shared. Every once in a while the silo will get too full, and it'll spill over, and the knowledge it contains may splash into the silo next to it. That's why serendipitous water cooler or coffee pot conversations are so important: they provide the only unstructured opportunity in most organizations for this spillage of wisdom and knowledge. Otherwise the left hand has no idea what the right hand is doing.

Ultimately, the org chart is a bulletproof vest that protects people from accountability. And even if you don't have an org chart, other aspects of your organization almost certainly have the same effect—surreptitiously insulating people from responsibility for what they *should* be doing, which is to create value for the organization and other people. Ultimately we have to create or provide something that's beneficial—and the ability to do that is what differentiates an entrepreneurial organization from a bureaucracy.

THE TRAGEDY OF MISDIRECTED HUMAN RESOURCES

Every organization has the potential for greatness. We all have the ability to be exceptional, but we can't get there if we limit ourselves to doing things a certain way just because we believe that we *should* do them that way. Our greatness comes from our uniqueness, which gets watered down when we allow our companies to become bureaucratized. What holds an organization back and keeps it from recognizing its potential is our attitude toward the teams we work with—and more important, the *individuals* we work with. Too many companies have a culture in which it's considered a badge of honor to be busy, regardless of *what* we're busy with, and regardless of what role we have in the organization. As a result, the most important asset any organization has—its people—gets squandered.

This happens because too many of those people don't fully understand what they're doing or why they're doing it, and too few of them are doing what they would truly love to be doing. None of this is the team members' fault; the problem is the organizational structure, which disconnects people from how their jobs fit into the organization as a whole.

Every organization has—or should have—two distinct realms within its structure: a "Front Stage," where the company interacts with its clientele, and a "Back Stage," where its product or service is produced. As an employee, the toughest situation to be in is being unsure whether you're in the public-facing Front Stage part of the organization or the private, Back Stage part, and what that position implies.

This problem is compounded by a widespread lack of respect for the private side of the organization, the Back Stage. Many Back Stage people believe there's more notoriety to be earned on the Front Stage, so they work to insert themselves into it . . . or they diminish and demoralize themselves by thinking they're not as valuable. The Back Stage jobs are seen as less important, less glamorous—and therefore less desirable. People are diminished within an organization through a lack of respect, and, in my experience, a lack of understanding of the importance of each of these arenas undermines the health, success, and greatness of an organization.

Conversely, the same thing can happen to organizations led by people who are exclusively Back Stage-oriented. They don't have any respect for the sales and marketing team, because they believe there's less substance there than in the operational realm or the delivery and production departments.

The biggest threat to our businesses isn't competition, regulation, or taxes, or even COVID-19. The greatest threat to our businesses is optics—how we perceive our job as leaders and our role in the organization. In this age of technology, instant responses, and manufactured urgencies, the most

CHAPTER 2

THE BIRTH OF THE O³ QUAD MOD

ENTREPRENEURSHIP IS NOT A PANACEA, IT ISN'T FOR EVERYBODY. Before you choose that path, make sure you know exactly what you're getting into. The point of going into business is to improve your life, and frankly, killing yourself from stress and overwork is no use to anybody.

- Hugh MacLeod

IT'S TIME TO RESTRUCTURE

Let's return now to that cold, dreary day at PDX airport. (If you don't know what I'm talking about, go back now and read that prologue you skipped!)

On that day, I realized that the organizational structure of my company needed to be completely reimagined. As I sat there and sketched out possible alternative arrangements, I started thinking about the importance of simplicity. The best teachers of concepts are the ones who can distill things down to a couple of sentences. Because I'm not very smart and I'm kind of lazy, when I'm faced with a problem I always seek solutions that are easy for me to understand. If I can easily understand an idea, then it's easy for me to communicate—and it's easy for other people to understand it.

I started with my frustration at the difficulty of constant multitasking. Many entrepreneurs are very proud of their ability to shift gears on the fly. Not me. I think it's a soul-sucking, ego-boosting, prideful attitude to have toward leadership and management. I knew I couldn't continue to have both hands in every single aspect of my business at all times.

When you go out and interact with the public in the places that create value for your organization—i.e., when you're on the Front Stage—you need to be confident that the wheels are not going to fall off the wagon in the back room while you're out there. You need to know that the commitments you make will be upheld because you've got processes, procedures, and systems in place to ensure consistent success. I knew we needed better processes, procedures, and systems from a Back Stage standpoint so we wouldn't have to reinvent the wheel every time a problem came up.

We also needed not to be relying on the strength of our personalities to impose our will as leaders and managers; instead of managing *people*, we needed to be managing *systems*. When you have good systems in place, then the people part of the equation takes better care of itself because you have a universal playbook, and everybody knows how they should respond to workflow, responsibilities, and problems when they come up.

This very simple question of how to assess regularly occurring issues was not being addressed by the leadership of my organization.

Dentists have a saying: "If your teeth are a problem, just ignore them . . . and eventually they'll go away." In business, if you ignore some of these issues that we're ultimately responsible for as leaders and managers, or if you don't make clear your expectations of how you want them to be dealt with to be consistent with your culture, then things will default to management of people instead of management of systems.

That was my big epiphany. The problem wasn't that we didn't have systems in place; it was that those systems weren't living up to the expectations I had for the culture of my organization. As a result, I was laboring under the inordinate burden of always having to respond to issues and crises on a moment's notice—and that was no longer acceptable.

Once I defined what I *didn't* want to do, I was able to work my way to a place where I could define the things that needed to be done and provide an organizational framework for *how* those things would get done. (It's intriguing to me that, when asked what you want, the answer is usually about all of the things you *don't* want! After letting the air out of that balloon, you can get on to what you *do* want.)

THE MEANING OF THE Q³ QUAD MOD

You're probably wondering about the name of this framework, the Q³ Quad Mod—what does it mean?

It's pretty simple, actually: The Q³ (Q-cubed) stands for the *quality* of three things: **people, purpose,** and **processes**. *Quad* is short for *quadrant* (as you'll soon see, the model is divided into four quadrants), and *Mod*, obviously, is short for *model*. (They're shortened because they rhyme that way, which makes them easier to remember—again, I'm not very smart and I'm kind of lazy!) For your organization to function well, your people, your purpose, and your processes all need to be of the highest quality to the core: highly ethical, value-oriented, and excellent. Notice I didn't say perfect, but excellent. And as I've learned as an architect, a design is never really done. The value of developing the Q³ Quad Mod is that it's not static—it's dynamic, with the ability to morph as your organization develops.

First, let's talk about the *quality of your people*. You need people who are dedicated to learning and growing. People who have integrity and credibility, who say what they do and do what they say. You need people who practice what Dan Sullivan calls "the referability habits": show up on time, finish what you start, do what you say, and say "please" and "thank you." You need people who are genuinely excited to be where they are in terms of their roles within the organization—whether that individual is the CEO or the person who changes the toner in the printers.

Part of it is just self-actualization. When people recognize the opportunities they have, then they become dedicated to lifelong learning and self-improvement. We always have reasons to think we've been held back, whether intellectually or financially, don't we? "I don't have the money, I don't have the resources, I don't have the time." That attitude does not serve anyone well; it breeds a victim mindset, and that doesn't have a place in the world of entrepreneurialism. If you're dedicated to self-improvement, you'll strive to make yourself better at whatever you do, whether you are sweeping floors or developing a cure for cancer. Patrick Lencioni wrote a great book called *The Ideal Team Player*, which we've encouraged our entire team to read and use to evaluate existing and potential team members. It creates a platform for the intuition we all have and helps to evolve and codify that phenomenon into a tangible process. The better we make ourselves, the more we invest in ourselves, the more impact we can have on society in general and in business, specifically. That's what I mean by "quality of people."

Quality of purpose means doing things for the right reasons. The goal of every business is to stay in business. That means you have to make money, right? But that can't be your only reason for being in business. Your purpose has to be to bring value to your stakeholders—your investors, your clientele, your employees, and yourself. To create value for people and for your market is to act with high quality of purpose.

Last, we have *quality of process*. Process is ultimately what this book is all about. The foundation for every organization is its processes. The more solidly an organization is built on a foundation of good practices, done for the right reasons with the right people, the more successful that organization will become. And these things are the intangibles with every organization; the public doesn't see them, but the way you approach the market is largely defined by the quality of the processes within your organization. To a creative person, processes might sound boring or limiting, but the reality is that consistent processes actually create *more* headspace and freedom to be creative. By systematizing things so you can say "this is how we do it," you can trust the system and free up your mind to solve problems, come up with new ideas, and create value for your clients. That's why processes are so important.

THE BASIC STRUCTURE OF THE Q³ QUAD MOD

Simply put, this model is divided into four quadrants—Marketing, Design, Operations, and Production—each of which sits within one of two hemispheres, the Front Stage and the Back Stage. The Front Stage is where value is created, and the Back Stage is where confidence is created.

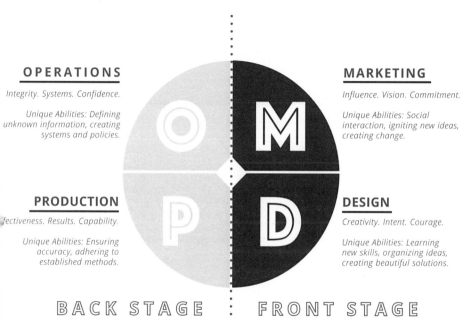

OPERATIONS

Integrity. Systems. Confidence.

Unique Abilities: Defining unknown information, creating systems and policies.

MARKETING

Influence. Vision. Commitment.

Unique Abilities: Social interaction, igniting new ideas, creating change.

PRODUCTION

fectiveness. Results. Capability.

Unique Abilities: Ensuring accuracy, adhering to established methods.

DESIGN

Creativity. Intent. Courage.

Unique Abilities: Learning new skills, organizing ideas, creating beautiful solutions.

BACK STAGE
Confidence Building

FRONT STAGE
Value Creation

THE FRONT STAGE

The Front Stage is the part of your organization that goes out to the world and represents what you do and how you do it. This is the domain that encompasses the Marketing and Design Quadrants:

The Marketing Quadrant. This, obviously, is the arena that covers sales functions, but there are other aspects of it too, including related considerations such as public relations and outreach.

The Design Quadrant. As with Marketing, the domain of the Design Quadrant appears obvious at first glance—it's the design of your product, right? That's certainly part of it, but the Design Quadrant also covers activities directly related to your branding, such as your logo, your packaging, how your product appears in advertisements, and so on. (This is why the Q^3 Quad Mod is equally applicable to service-oriented businesses that don't necessarily make a physical product.)

All the things you do that relate to your brand are represented in the design of your organization and whatever it is you're delivering. I'm not even talking at this point about the essence of whatever service or product you're offering; rather, I'm talking about how that service or product is packaged, about how the world sees your initial presentation of what you're providing to your clients or the market.

THE BACK STAGE

Behind the Front Stage, less visible but no less important, is the Back Stage. This is where the sausage is made. It is where all your internal processes operate, out of the public view. The Back Stage is the domain of the propeller heads. It's where you'll find the nerdy people with pocket protectors who make everything you do possible. (You only find the pocket-protector people at engineering firms though, not at architectural firms!)

The Back Stage comprises the Production and Operations Quadrants:

The Production Quadrant. As its name implies, the Production Quadrant is where you actually produce the work for your clientele. In a manufacturing enterprise, for example, this would be the plant at which your widgets are actually manufactured.

The Operations Quadrant. Operations is even deeper Back Stage than production. That's where you'll find accounts payable, accounts receivable, and human resources. The health of most organizations can be determined by looking at what goes on in their Operations Quadrant.

A BALANCING ACT

In Chapter 1, I noted that many organizations place undue emphasis on either the Front Stage or the Back Stage, to the detriment of both (a subject we'll discuss at greater length in Chapter 3). Unfortunately, because of the way many organizations are led, it's also common for companies to place too much emphasis on one quadrant at the expense of the others.

The image below shows you what an organization's four quadrants look like when they're out of balance. In this example, as you can see, the Operations Quadrant is given short shrift in this hypothetical company; maybe it's underfunded or understaffed . . . or maybe management simply doesn't pay enough attention to the departments within that quadrant.

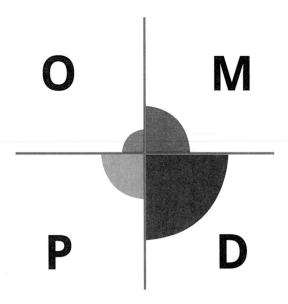

Conversely, the Design Quadrant takes up an inordinate amount of the company's resources. This may mean that some people working in the Design Quadrant ought to be in production or marketing. Or it could mean that the design people have a disproportionate share of power within the organization—i.e., they have built a silo—and it's a big one.

When there's an imbalance in the significance of each quadrant, what follows is a breakdown in how they work together. In a healthy organization, you can almost draw a

ver your crib when you were a baby in order to
you into going to sleep. It's got to be balanced . .
etic and needs to be able to move too. Similarly,
your organization will move and shift like a m
manipulated by the wind: everything changes, bu
in balance. If the mobile is not in balance, then i
and breaks.

n the healthiest organization will often have a he

CHAPTER 3

THE THEATER OF OPERATIONS: FRONT STAGE VS. BACK STAGE

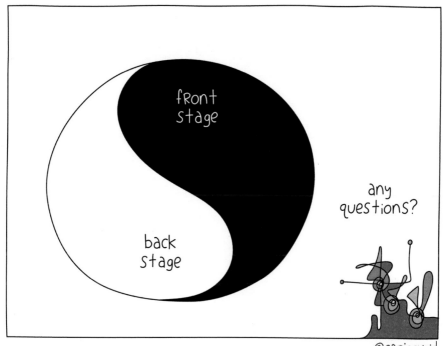

THE FRONT STAGE AND THE BACK STAGE ARE VERY DIFFERENT WORLDS, AND YET THEY'RE NOT.

Same but different. Different but the same.

- Hugh MacLeod

SEEING THROUGH THE CURTAIN

The notion of dividing a company into Front and Back Stage arenas isn't new. The concept originates, of course, in the theater: the Front Stage and Back Stage areas are, respectively, what the audience sees and what it doesn't see.

When you go to see a play, you expect to lose yourself, to become immersed in a fictional story that you absorb as though it were a series of real events actually happening to people you know. This is how you become invested in the story—it's what makes the "magic" of the theater possible.

But what happens if the curtain separating the Front Stage from the Back Stage is accidentally opened a few inches? You'll see actors and stagehands rushing back and forth, distracting you and taking you out of the story the theater company worked so hard to bring to life. If you're sitting close enough, you may even see actors changing costumes and putting on makeup. The illusion is spoiled, and with it the magic—and your experience.

The simplest illustration of how this works in the business world can be seen at an auto repair shop. Most shops do not allow customers in the work area. They say the rule is "for insurance reasons," and maybe there's some truth to that . . . but insurance isn't the only reason, and it's likely not even the primary one.

No, the real reason customers are barred from the shop area can be summed up by the novelty sign hanging in the customer waiting area: "Our rate is $75 an hour. If you watch, it's $100 an hour. If you help, it's $200 an hour."

The tone of this sign is lighthearted, but its purpose is very serious: to keep the Front and Back Stages of the shop separate, and to keep the customer out of the Back Stage. Certainly there's a time and a place for the public—the Front Stage constituents for whom we produce things—to be involved with what's being produced for them, but it's rarely during the production phase of the work.

Of course I noted in the last chapter that the lines between quadrants can sometimes be necessarily blurry, and the same is sometimes true of the line between Front Stage and Back Stage. The cashiers who take your money when you come to pick up your car may not know much about engines, and even if they do, they're not the ones who worked on your brake problem. So they may call the mechanic who did the work and have him come to the front office area to answer your questions. But if some of your questions concern the shop's prices, the mechanic may look to the cashier or the manager rather than answer you himself.

RESPECTING AND UNDERSTANDING EVERYONE'S ROLES

When you're on the Front Stage, you're putting on your best face and putting your best foot forward. You're showing the public what you're capable of, and you're doing it in a very purposeful way. To do that well, you have to feel confident about the value you're offering, and for that you need a Back Stage that under-stands the value of the Front Stage—those representatives of the organization who are out interacting with the public.

By the same token, the Front Stage needs to respect the work of the Back Stage—which too often it doesn't. A friend of mine works for one of the "big eight" accounting firms. It's a multina-tional company, and she has a very high-level job in what would be classified under the Q^3 Model as the Production Quadrant. She worked with the sales-and-marketing vice president to develop a model that the sales team could use to better describe the services the company delivers, in terms of value.

Because of her specific expertise, her contribution to this project was utterly invaluable. And yet, that sales guy didn't have any respect for what she did—even though he himself had worked with her to create this model. He tried to intimidate her into letting him water down her contribution, and he ended up using the model in a way that benefited him personally more than it benefited the organization.

This is the kind of thing that can happen in a company that does not understand the value of the Back Stage. Within my organization, before I devised this new organizational model, that value needed to be clarified because the Front Stage didn't have a lot of respect for the Back Stage. I've noticed this problem in a lot of organizations: a lack of sufficient understanding and respect between the sales people and the production and operations people. The translation from one hemisphere to the other—the understanding of what each hemisphere did— needed to be improved. The Back Stage people needed to believe that the Front Stage folks were aware of the challenges inherent in their work. The Front Stage, on the other hand, needed to feel confident that the Back Stage wouldn't balk at supporting them when they promised delivery timelines.

The single biggest rub between the Front Stage and the Back Stage is the promise of delivery time. If you're on the Front Stage, you recognize that there's a shelf life on your ability to close a contract, and sometimes you may even want to bring a

Back Stage person along to the meeting so that if any technical questions come up, that person is there to answer them. The Front Stage shouldn't be writing checks that the Back Stage can't cash, but the Back Stage needs to be willing to honor whatever checks the Front Stage deems it necessary to write. Otherwise it undermines the people who are the public face of your company. There will be plenty of time to argue about Front Stage promises later, back at the office, when you're all together Back Stage in the collective stew that is your organization, and can afford to let the line between the stages get a bit blurry.

But it needs to be a hard, fast line when you're out there in the trenches.

It's crucial to remember that each of us is an important part of the organization we work for. It doesn't matter who you are within the organization; we all work here, and if you can step outside yourself—out of this idea that it's all about you, the individual—then everyone benefits. If I help make the organization successful, I myself will therefore be successful in turn, and we'll all get to a much better place—a place of camaraderie, collaboration, success, and results.

At my company, an interesting little drama often plays out when we've just done some preliminary design and we're in a meeting with the client. The meeting will include someone from marketing, someone from design, and someone from production. The design people find that they have to shift from somewhat of a sales role to somewhat of a production role because now we've enticed the client; we've impressed them with our ability to provide what they want, and now they're invested. They're intrigued . . . and they want more. They want to know: *When can we get to the next phase?*

Production people will think about all the things on their desk right now, and all the things on their calendar . . . and being only human, sometimes they will begin to think more of themselves than the organization. They will try to buy themselves as much time as they can because by nature, they *have* to: they live in a world of deadlines and budgets. Meanwhile, the people on the Front Stage are there to try to close the deal and get things to the next level.

So how should this seeming misalignment of incentives be handled? The right answer would be for the Front Stage person to say to the client, "When do you need this done? What would be best for you? OK, let me go back and talk to the team and work with them to determine how we can meet your goals." Then commit to a schedule to achieve that deadline. You're still making a commitment, but without undermining your Back Stage team.

Back Stage team members, if they're present at the meeting, respond out of fear and try to buy themselves as much time as they can, nervously blurting out, "Six months." And once that comes out of someone's mouth—as soon as someone sandbags a deadline—you know the client is out. I've seen it happen. And all the work you've done to reach the point where you can sign a contract for the majority of the work, which is yet to be done—it all goes out the window. That one statement is all it takes for the client to conclude that you don't really care about them, and all because the production person spoke out of fear and sandbagged a deadline. I've seen arguments, both as the architect and as a purchaser of services, that drove people to leave the conference room because there was so much tension between the Front Stage and Back Stage people.

The way to show respect in both directions is this: On the Front Stage, as much as possible, you say, "Let me go back and check with the team." And on the Back Stage, you defer to the person who's representing you on the Front Stage. Understand your role, and remember that the Front Stage person has to be able to say credibly, "We have an amazing team that we can mobilize to meet your deadlines as soon as everything is in place."

The toughest negotiation to have is the one you don't know you're having. It is a negotiation until you get that final contract signed. It is a negotiation until you move things from the Front to the Back Stage. You have to understand as a Back Stage person that until the deal's done, there are a lot of variables. The scope must be defined. Services need to be articulated, and fees have to be agreed to. A whole bunch of stuff is yet to be done, and as a Back Stage person you can avoid sabotaging that effort by understanding that—by saying to yourself, "You know what, this may be a tough deadline or it may not. A lot of things are going to change, and I have plenty of time to freak out, so I'm not going to freak out now. I'm going to trust that the person who's leading this meeting has enough respect for me to recognize that I can't plan a manned mission to Mars in a week."

Now, when there's not enough respect between the two stages, what happens is that the people on the Front Stage will say *anything* to seal the deal. This makes the Back Stage more intractable, less willing to work to provide a creative solution. I have seen fights break out when a marketing person or design person comes back and tells the people overseeing production about all the things they committed to without checking in with the group.

And the biggest offenders are the lead entrepreneurs. Why? Because they know what they could have done themselves when the organization was small, and so they foist those expectations onto people who are part of what is now a much bigger organization. What happens then? Those people dig their heels in, and you get disruption and erosion in the culture you're trying to create.

TIME AND PLACE

One way to avoid this kind of problem is to foster a culture in which everyone understands the concept of *time and place*. That's a cornerstone of the Q^3 Quad Mod—being in the right time and the right place to have the right conversation.

I hate to say it, but people in the Back Stage are not exactly known for their people skills, unless they work in HR, or they're a leader of a quadrant (like a really good CFO, for example). That's not a knock against the Back Stage; it's just that the nature of what they do tends to select for a different personality type.

This was certainly the problem with my erstwhile financial director, who called me that day while I was stuck at the Portland airport. He'd chosen a really bad moment to call me about a problem that I was—at that moment—in no position to deal with.

Obviously, an entrepreneur needs to be accessible to the team, but no one can be expected to be available at any time and any place. And if my financial director had had any sense of time and place, he would have chosen a better moment to bring up a problem.

It's a distorted sense of self—or maybe more accurately, a distorted sense of self-importance—that causes this problem. If you lack imagination and empathy, you won't think about the other person's time, or what their role may require of them, and this lack of mutual understanding will creep into every interaction you have with that person. So you won't think twice about calling your boss with a problem while he's waiting for a plane at an airport gate—or about sandbagging a promise the sales manager has just made, right in front of the client he's just made it to.

At any given time, we have a limited capacity to address any given issue. To be at our best in whatever quadrant we're working in at that time, we need to be able to focus. And for that to be possible, everyone on the team needs to understand everyone else's roles within the organization. Only then will they be able to determine the best time and place to have any given conversation.

Ensuring that all team members understand this concept of time and place helps to sow mutual respect, which in turn improves how we all function in our respective roles.

RESPECTING YOUR OWN ROLE

Our culture in the US has done a marvelous job of creating an environment in which people believe they're falling short. The way we as a society are experiencing that feeling of inadequacy is through comparisons, and social media is a reflection of that unhealthy comparison culture. It presents an idealized version of who we are and who other people are, which gives rise to a feeling of inadequacy within ourselves.

Our educational system contributes to this as well, from elementary school all the way up to the college level. I think there's a great desire on the part of some of the people in charge of these systems to have us all be the same shade of gray—to make us all the same. We're living in this amorphous society in which we can all feel good in our mediocrity, and it's just not who we're created to be. That's not who people are. It's a lie being foisted on young people: look at all the eleventh-place ribbons and participation trophies in sporting events in which nobody keeps score anymore. That is not a cornerstone of—and pardon me if this sounds a little bit corny—American greatness. The reason we're the greatest country on the planet in terms of our ability to invent things and advance people is our basic understanding that we all have unique gifts.

In business school, you learn how to identify the seven traits of a leader, and when you learn this you may realize that you're deficient in two of them—but you're off-the-charts excellent in another one. Most students respond to this revelation by obsessively focusing on the traits they're deficient in rather than making the most of the exceptional character qualities they're more abundantly gifted with. As a result, they end up spending so much time and focus on their natural shortcomings—and so little time cultivating their strengths—that all they manage to achieve is a high level of general mediocrity. We take our best talents and dilute them to the point where everything is now on the same level. And so that gift that we have, our uniqueness, gets watered down.

This doesn't make us unemployable: we can still get a great job, and we can integrate into an organization, but in very short order we're going to be burned out because we're not using our talents in the right way. We're going to be doing what we *think* we should be doing, or what we're being told to do by people who think they have a better understanding than we do of what our capabilities are.

One thing I really want to advocate in this book is self-respect. As I said in Chapter 1, many Back Stage people see the work that's done on the Front Stage as having less substance, less value than their own work. Conversely, many people on both stages see Back Stage work as less glamorous or less important because so much of it goes unseen. People need to understand that they have unique qualities that are different from everybody else's. Smart organizations recognize these distinct capabilities and allow people to develop them so they can use them on a really high level within the organization . . . and then they hire other people with complementary talents. By exploiting all of its employees' unique abilities in a positive way, a business prospers.

The road to unhappiness is littered with comparisons. That's what's so insidious about social media: it compares us to other people, and the unhappiness and dissatisfaction it breeds in our society is now bleeding over into the business world and manifesting in feelings of inadequacy in comparison to people with different gifts. Here's the thing: showing up and doing your job with excellence is enough. The talents you have are enough. Build upon that by considering ways to help the team be better and not making it *all about you* and you will increase your satisfaction exponentially. Your job is no less important just because the client doesn't know your name.

CHAPTER 4

THE MARKETING QUADRANT

IN THE END, OBJECTS DON'T MAKE US HAPPY, RELATIONSHIPS MAKE US HAPPY. No matter how much you love your stuff, your stuff can't love you back. In the end, the value a company creates is in the relationships, not in the wires, pipes, bricks, and mortar.

- Hugh MacLeod

VALUING YOUR NETWORK

People do business with people; they don't do business with contacts.

That understanding is the nucleus of every good marketing program. I deal with a lot of clients who throw me in front of lenders, both for debt and for equity, and when you read the ads run by some of the equity people out there—which I do from time to time—they all celebrate the people involved in the deal: "We just did a $50 million deal, and Joe and Jane and Sue were instrumental in putting it together."

When you look closely at these people, however, they all seem like they were fairly tangential to getting the deal done . . . but they have been thrust onto the Front Stage because of the quality of what they were able to achieve together. I marvel at how these lenders connect those dots: "Who do you know? Do you know so and so at XYZ Equity? I did a deal with them last year, and they were phenomenal."

And it works the other way, too: "Do you know so and so at that other firm? The people they put out there on the front line are a bunch of arrogant young knuckleheads who think they know everything, but they really don't know *anything*."

So the importance of your network—the *people* in the network, not just the contacts—can't be underestimated.

WHAT'S YOUR STORY?

The Marketing Quadrant is the umbrella that covers the sales department, but it involves other aspects too, including related considerations like public relations and outreach. And these activities have to be reinforced by high-quality people, processes, and purpose.

Chelsea and I were at a conference a couple of years ago, and five of the biggest lenders in the country were there, represented by the senior people within those organizations—the ones who decide who gets money for new development deals and who doesn't. These people have very active roles in their institutions, despite their seniority, and they were conducting something like a mini *Shark Tank*—you pitched your deal and they decided whether to lend you the money to do it.

Naturally, if they were going to lend you money, they wanted certain information: they wanted financials of course, but they also wanted to know that you had good processes that supported the numbers you were putting out. After that, the next important determinant was the quality of your organization—the quality of your people.

But the question that mattered to them most was: *What are you trying to do? Why are you trying to do it? Whom are you trying to serve? What benefit will you bring to the consumer?* In a nutshell, those three Qs that I mentioned in Chapter 2—quality people, quality processes, and quality purpose—were the governing criteria they used to evaluate your organization and determine whether you were going to get their money.

I tell this story not just because it ties in neatly with my "three Qs," but because the last and most important of them— quality of purpose—is foundational to any marketing strategy. You need to communicate, not just to investors but to your prospective clientele, *why* you're in the business you're in. You need to be able to articulate, with passion and conviction, what value you're bringing to the table. What benefit are you going to bring to your clients or customers? What problem are you trying to solve? How will the world be a better place as a result of people doing business with you?

The real secret sauce of your organization is why you do what you do—what impact you want to make and what kind of people you have doing the work. The whole needs to be greater than the sum of its parts.

NO ONE CARES WHAT YOU KNOW

When I started work on this book, my editor and I sat down to discuss my objectives, and he asked an important question—what problems did I want to help the reader address? In reply, I said something about helping entrepreneurs liberate themselves from various unproductive mindsets.

"What mindsets are unproductive?" he asked.

Being self-centered is the first one, I told him. Most of us think of ourselves first. If you want to be successful in life, understanding what's important to other people is the first step. It's a cliché that's been beaten nearly to death, but it's worth repeating here because it's true: *people don't care how much you know until they know how much you care.* That's a simplified way of saying that I might have something great to sell, but I'm just a solution in search of a problem—a hammer in search of a nail—until I find out what's important to *you.*

I was thirty-six the first and only time I got married. Before that, when I was single, I dedicated myself to finding the *right* spouse. I didn't want to jump into the wrong kind of marriage and find myself divorced after five years, as happens to so many people.

In the course of my dating life, I learned something significant that also applies to how I built my business. When I sat with dates over drinks or dinner, I'd ask questions and listen closely to the responses. I wanted to know what was important to them, what they valued, where they wanted their lives to take them. In every one of those conversations, 75 percent of the talking was being done by the woman on the other side of the table. And when the evening was over, regardless of whatever else those women may have thought about me, they all shared one impression: they thought I was a lot smarter and more attractive because I asked them questions and listened.

Once I took that lesson to heart, it wasn't much of a stretch to apply it to my professional life. When I go to an initial meeting to establish a new business relationship, I ask a few questions . . . and then I sit back and listen. Not only do I make this a habit myself; I've inculcated it into the culture of my company. And because of that, people think we're really, *really* smart— but the reality is that we're just really good at discerning what's important to the people sitting across the table.

That talent serves us in two ways: First, it enables us to maintain a reputation for caring about our clients. Second, it helps us to maintain our awareness of what people want in general, so we're never out of touch with the public's ever-changing tastes.

Every organization has a story about why it does what it does. The problem is that the organization thinks it has to present itself in a certain way. We've been told, "*This* is what the stakeholders want to hear"—without having actually asked them.

When you have your first kickoff meeting with a new client, it's natural to want to talk at length about your unique strengths and accomplishments—and often your client's eyes glaze over. That's because a lot of marketing and sales professionals have a predilection for self-aggrandizement: "We've done this, we've done that. We've worked for this one, we've worked for that one. We, we, we; I, I, I." If I'm sitting there as the one who is going to sign the check or the contract you're putting in front of me, and you haven't once asked me what is important to me—how do you think I'm apt to respond?

AUTHENTICITY

I'm sure I don't need to define *authenticity* for you. You know what that word means, and it's something you look for in your dealings with other people, both personal and professional.

But do you offer it in return?

Your first impulse may be to snort indignantly, "Of course we do!" And yet, far too many organizations make doing business with them an utterly impersonal—and therefore inauthentic—experience.

You see this when you go into any bank branch. The teller greets you cheerfully: "Hi, how's it going today? Got any big plans for the weekend?"

"Yeah, I was going to cook up some crystal meth this weekend and maybe give a little taste to my kids."

"Oh that sounds great! Hope you have a good time!"

"Yeah, that's why I need so many singles and twenties right now—because, you know, my business is very much cash-oriented."

"Oh OK, no problem, we can get those for you."

I mean, seriously . . . no matter what you say to them, *that's* the conversation! They have learned to ask two or three questions, but they don't know why they are asking them, they don't really care, and they certainly aren't listening.

Another form of inauthenticity is the use of psychologically manipulative tactics to makes sales. I recently bought a new luxury car and the sales process was so awful it was embarrassing. What they said, essentially, was, "We're doing you a favor by selling you this car, because no one else is getting one." The tactic is called "limited availability" or "scarcity" marketing—you'd better buy it now, and you should be happy that I'm selling it to you. There are still people out there who sell that way, but it's a disrespectful, ineffective way to sell, and a lousy way to deal with people in general.

It's oddly reminiscent of "negging," a sneaky, unethical seduction technique devised about twenty years ago and promulgated in a rash of books by self-styled "pickup artists." Essentially the idea is, when you are out with a woman, to pepper your conversation with subtle putdowns—innocent-sounding but slightly negative remarks that undermine her self-esteem and position yourself as somebody whose approval she should crave. It seldom works in the real world, but effective or not, it's despicable . . . and the kinds of sales techniques they tried on me in that dealership are no different in principle.

We could do a whole book on bad sales techniques. My point in bringing up some of these tactics is to emphasize how disingenuous they are—how *inauthentic*—and to warn you about damage they can do to the credibility of your business. An organization that is clear about its purpose will be concerned about the quality of its people, and won't tolerate dishonest, manipulative, and inauthentic sales tactics.

The last bit of advice I have for you on the subject of authenticity is a bit counterintuitive—in fact, if somebody had told me forty years ago that I would ever do this in a sales or marketing environment, I would have said, "You've got the wrong guy." But sometimes the best thing you can do to protect the legitimacy of your brand is to say, "You know what? Now that we've taken the time to discuss your needs . . . I don't think we're the right organization for you. I don't think that what we do can be of benefit to you, but I can refer you to another organization that may be a better fit."

Everyone who works in that Marketing Quadrant, whether they are in sales or marketing or PR, must be able to do this. If you feel ill at ease in a meeting, you should consider the possibility that it may be because you know your organization can't do a good job with the project you're being asked to undertake. Maybe it's something you've never done before; or maybe you've done it before and it's not gone well. Or maybe you just don't feel a good alignment with the people and your gut is telling you to walk away. Regardless of the reason, you need to be able to say to a prospective new client, "I don't think we're right for you. It's just not a good fit."

If you can't or won't do this, what happens? You take on a project your company is ill-suited to complete, something that's not in your wheelhouse. And at best, if nothing goes wrong (and something always does!), you get paid for doing a B-minus job without anyone appreciating how difficult it was to get it done at all. At worst, everything goes sideways, and now you have an angry client and a damaged reputation. Either way, it doesn't benefit your market and it doesn't benefit your organization.

Being crystal clear about who you are is part of having a quality purpose platform within your organization. Tricks like "negging," as juvenile as they may seem, sometimes actually work in the dating environment—and the reason is that the people who are susceptible to them don't know who they are, deep down. They don't have an identity other than what the world has told them their identity should be—and I think a lot of businesses are that way, too. Businesses are like people, and people tend to develop a certain impression of what they are trying to bring forth into the world; they don't want to ever be told that they can't work in any given environment.

Some salespeople will do *anything* to make a sale. Many of them have taken sales classes that teach skills like how to overcome objections—but if you are really a talented salesperson, you should be able to make authentic connections with people, and your primary objective should be to do what's right for your organization, your client, and your market. That's a much more meaningful way to approach sales, because better quality people improve the quality of their relationships—by doing business with people, not with contacts.

When you are being authentic, everything is about the other person. Most salespeople have the hardest time doing one thing that would distinguish them from 90 percent of the sales professionals out there: just shut up and listen. And make a few notes. And then—wait for it—actually follow up as promised, in a timely manner!

THE RELATIONSHIPS BETWEEN QUADRANTS

The real strength of the Q³ Quad Mod lies in how the individual quadrants work together. So let's talk about that for a minute.

I consider myself to be a designer and an architect, but I also have a foundational role as the spokesperson for my organization, which means I've worked within all four quadrants of my company. What I've learned from that experience is that a marketing person doesn't exist only in that quadrant. One of the strengths of the Q³ Quad Mod that distinguishes it from an organizational chart is the fact that the marketing person is encouraged to have conversations with people in the other quadrants. They're expected to treat all interactions, both with the people in the backroom and those on the public side of the organization, like they are marketing interactions—not in a sales sense, but in terms of treating their colleagues respectfully by listening to them. We want our marketing people not to speak in sales jargon when talking to design people. We want them not to get irritated when they occasionally have to explain some of the details of their roles, and we want them to listen well to the people in the Back Stage of the organization.

This brings us back to the "quality people" part of Q³. Part of your job is making sure everyone on your team gets the same respect that you would bring to your dealings with somebody on the Front Stage. That deference doesn't mean you're not going to be involved in the sausage-making; it simply means that when you go outside your quadrant, you have to take the time to start from the beginning in some ways. In short, how you treat people is an important part of how the model works.

Marketing doesn't just happen on the public side of a company. When I began to treat the Back Stage team members in my organization like they were on the public side, I showed up differently as a CEO. My interest in them empowered them, and it led to a new practice in our organization, a thing we call Behind the Build.

Behind the Build is me interviewing our team members, asking them about what is important to them within the organization and in life. It has increased their engagement with their work and their connection to our organization, and it has helped us create a culture that is very family-like (but in a non-cultish way). We like to say we took the *cult* out of *culture*. That's important to us, because some organizations make it weird to work for them—like Walmart, for example, which makes all its employees start every shift with a big, creepy "Walmart Cheer."

The air travel industry has a thing called Crew Resource Management, or CRM. The idea was introduced in the late 1970s to minimize the danger of catastrophic human error by making the culture in airplane cockpits less authoritarian.

Before CRM, you might have a person sitting in the pilot seat who was a gray-haired professional with thousands of hours of experience—and a copilot whose job was to *sit there, shut up, get the coffee, and put the flaps and the landing gear down when I tell you.* That was it. "I don't need you to think, and I don't need you to tell me what you think I should do. Sit there, shut up, and do what I tell you and nobody will get hurt." And if the copilot noticed that the fuel warning light was going off, he might not say anything to the pilot because . . . well, he's the pilot—the captain—and he knows everything. The captain is omnipotent, so I don't dare say anything because if I do, I'm going to get my hand slapped.

You may remember Asiana Airlines Flight 214, a perfectly good jet with absolutely no mechanical problems that crashed at San Francisco International airport on a bluebird day in 2013. The five pilots on board, one of whom was an instructor, watched the pilot go under the glide slope—the path that guides you electronically to the end of the runway—and said nothing. His air speed began deteriorating, and at least one or two of the other pilots saw this happen . . . and said nothing. Two people were killed, and 168 were injured.[1]

Crew Resource Management says that if you're on the plane and you have a pulse, you speak up if you see something that looks wrong. That includes flight attendants. If you feel the hair on the back of your neck going up because something is rattling in a way it doesn't usually rattle, it's your responsibility to go to the flight crew and say, "This doesn't seem right." Everybody has the responsibility to speak up.

That's the model that we use when we have meetings, and if a culture like that had been in place at the CDC or the WHO back in February of 2020, important steps might have been taken that could have saved tens of thousands of lives. It doesn't matter if you've been with the organization for a week or fifteen years; it's your responsibility to say, "This doesn't look right," or "It could be a little bit better," or "I did this the way I was told and I didn't get the results I think we were looking for."

In a truly successful entrepreneurial organization, everybody has the same values, and those values get shared via culture. Whether you are on the public side or the private side, you have to be accustomed to asking questions and listening. If you are on the Back Stage, you need to see the people on the Front Stage as stakeholders in your success, and vice versa.

All marketing and outreach starts with an awareness of who you are (i.e., what your brand is), but more important than that is your awareness of other people. What is important to them?

Sitting here in the Operations Quadrant, I may ask, "Hey, Chelsea, did you just come back from a marketing meeting with XYZ company? What did they say?"

"Well," she might reply, "they said they want to do their next three projects with us because they admire the way we deal with tough problems and manage the process."

If I'm in operations, all of a sudden I know that my colleague has taken a little pressure off me by dint of her performance in that meeting. We're going to be getting three new projects with client XYZ because we ask good questions, have a culture of problem-solving, and have a great process—three things that boost my confidence that my contributions matter. And this series of events was possible because we have a structure that allows us to meet on a regular basis to ask these questions.

The implication of the traditional org chart is a vertical line that goes from the sales team to the assistant sales manager, and then another line to the sales manager, and then a complex set of additional lines connecting all these subsets of the sales and marketing department. The danger of the org chart is that you don't have a sales force out there representing the company; what you have instead is a bunch of salespeople out there representing *parts* of the company, which further segments your organization and creates more of these little silos.

The model I prefer to silos is baskets: within the marketing basket, you've got these little spheres that are all rubbing up against each other, sharing knowledge, and even sharing responsibilities when necessary. It's a little bit more work to have a Marketing Quadrant that is connected like this, but when you do it, the results can be astounding. Now all of a sudden, in what was supposed to be a typical sales training environment, the salespeople become one another's trainers.

So that quadrant doesn't need to be led by a series of steps up the org chart. Instead, you can throw all the ingredients together into this basket to make a stew, and then everything has the same flavor—the same culture. Even though you yourself may be a carrot and not an onion, you are all helping to flavor the same pot of food, and you are able to do that because you simmer together.

and *how*. That is, we had to answer all those quest

t was the point of departure for all our meeting age

mple way of distilling what the essence of the me

be. How many meetings have we all gone to wher

red, *What are we trying to do here? Why are we h*

everyone together in a basket rather than locked

silos brings quality of purpose to our meetings.

CHAPTER 5

THE DESIGN QUADRANT

GOOD DESIGN IS NEVER DONE, GOOD DESIGN NEVER STOPS. Good design affects everything at its core, informs everything you do. Good design is not something you hire or pay extra for. Good design is a philosophy, a way of being.

- Hugh MacLeod

YES . . . YOU HAVE IT TOO

Every organization has a Design Quadrant . . . even yours.

If you run a service-oriented business—say, a law firm—you may be thinking this chapter doesn't apply to you, since you don't make a product that needs to be designed in the way that an apartment building, a car, a piece of software, or a widget has to be designed. But I mean for the Q^3 Quad Mod to be universally applicable, and design is a broader concept than you may realize.

As I said in Chapter 2, the Design Quadrant encompasses things like branding activities, your logo, and anything else connected to your purposeful public presentation of yourself. The work of real-estate professionals, for example, has a design element: they consider staging, the appearance of the house they're showing. They may have a professional photographer take pictures of the house, rather than doing it themselves with an iPhone. They may put a batch of cookies in the oven to bake, so that the air is permeated with a smell that the prospective buyer associates with "home." All this activity is design.

Seen from this perspective, the Design Quadrant's intimate relationship with the Marketing Quadrant—the other half of the Front Stage—is obvious.

HOW TO REFINE AN IMPERFECT DESIGN

Much of what the Design Quadrant does—or *should* be doing—is marketing-related. The two activities often go hand in hand, and one of the best examples of this is the manner in which tech companies improve the design of their products by actually bringing them to market.

Consider how frequently this happens: you're working on a project, and suddenly there's a glitch in the application you're using. Or maybe the program even crashes. What happens after that? A little window pops up asking you for feedback. Or maybe it just asks you to allow it to send an automated report. Either way, the design of the product is flawed, and you, the consumer, are being asked to contribute to the company's ongoing efforts to identify and fix those flaws. You're helping the manufacturer with beta testing.

Companies do it with hardware too—as you know all too well if you're one of those people who just *has* to have the newest iPhone the very day it comes out. The complaints always begin to appear online that same day: "It won't charge while it's in sleep mode," or "The reception is terrible," or "The Wi-Fi isn't as fast as the model I had before." And then the next iteration of the product is better.

Why does this always happen? Because Apple and Microsoft are not interested in wasting an inordinate amount of time and money to perfect their products before they bring them to the public.

How organizations engage with their clients during the design phase has everything to do with their clients' perceptions of them: Software companies engage by creating flawed, buggy products and letting the most eager members of the public beta test them. The auto industry designs "concept cars" to display at auto shows to showcase new styling or new technology. The fashion industry puts runway models into outlandish, attention-getting outfits that no one is ever going to buy or wear to their sister's wedding.

But then they get feedback from the public. The auto manufacturers and fashion designers alike take note of what design elements got a positive reception at the last show, and these elements then show up in the products they actually sell.

Your own expectations and the market's expectations are two different things, and sometimes the only way to give the market what it wants is to first give it something it doesn't want. The alternative is to allow yourself to get hung up in the design phase indefinitely, always striving for perfection.

PERFECT IS THE ENEMY OF GOOD ENOUGH

I mentioned in Chapter 1 that the traditional org chart model serves to insulate people from responsibility for what they really *should* be doing. In some companies, one result of this insulation is that everything is endlessly worked on and nothing ever gets done.

When I was a young aspiring architect at the University of Arizona, one of my professors told us, "It takes two people to do an architectural rendering: one to actually do the work, and the second one to say *stop*." But when your org chart is so complex as to insulate everyone from responsibility to accomplish anything, it isn't anyone's job to say *stop* . . . so no one ever does until it's too late. It becomes everyone's full-time occupation to deflect questions and pretend they know what's going on. Endless meetings are held, but final decisions are never made; or if they are made, they're never implemented. Everyone is busy, but few are productive.

Here's a story that illustrates this: My business coach works with a lot of small businesses. A while back he was working with a software engineering company that had invested a couple million dollars in the development of an exciting new program. The product initially was meant to spend two years in development . . . but by the time my coach stepped in, it was now three years in the making, and the resources were dwindling. He told the clients, "You really need to get this to the market." And they replied, "It's not perfect yet. It's not perfect yet. It's not perfect yet."

It never did get perfect. They ended up going out of business and owing a whole bunch of venture capitalists the keys to their houses and their cars.

The point of this story is that it's possible—easy, in fact—to overbake a cake. There's a reason why you time something when you bake it, and the same principle applies in business. You can overbake an idea, a product, or a process, and when you overbake it, you've ruined it. The overbaked cake is dry and flavorless; the overbaked business product has missed its moment—the marketplace that demanded the product has changed, and the season is past, so nobody wants it. Too many businesses fail because their philosophy is "It's not done till it's overdone."

While this has always been true, the world we live in today has more urgent expectations than even five years ago, and the pace of innovation and change is only increasing. This makes the consequences of overbaking and inflexibility ever more dire.

My brother-in-law is a brilliant craftsman. He designs and builds beautiful furniture, and he's built wonderful things for my kids—skateboards, skimboards (like a surfboard, but smaller and without fins), and more. He also has a carpet-laying business, and just like a true craftsman—like a true designer—he has a certain way that he does it. Perfection matters to him. His takes a little bit longer to install carpet than most other carpet layers do, but the work is much, much better.

The problem is that his perfectionism goes largely unappreciated. Most customers don't care if their carpet has an extra seam in a place where nobody can see it. Their attitude is *just get this done so I can have my carpet for my party this weekend*. So the value of his idealism eventually reaches a point of diminishing returns.

Microsoft understands this. Apple understands this. They know that the development of software and phones is an iterative process, not a perfect one. And the public, by and large, understands that their participation in this process is both necessary and empowering for them.

Of course, rushing an imperfect product to market isn't necessarily the best strategy for all types of businesses. It's usually a mistake to take product development too far on the Front Stage before you get the client's authorization and approval of the concept. We often see competitors show up with finished drawings during the design phase, and I always think, *"Oh, you poor sap. You're going to get blown out of the water because what you are showing is way out of alignment with what the client is asking for; it's not the right time and place to be showing that to them."*

Really good organizations understand how to embrace the challenge of bringing a deliverable service or product to market—and how to balance that with the need to get input on it before it's finished. And that, ideally, is what design should do.

CROSS-QUADRANT RELATIONSHIPS

The relationship between marketing and design is profound, but the Design Quadrant also relates closely to the Production Quadrant: just as you can't market a product without understanding the design process, you can't design a product in the first place without having some sensitivity to how you will manufacture, build, document, or assess it.

So the lines between the quadrants often blur, even if the line between the Front and Back Stage is hard and fast. The design phase of any project is a series of problem-solving opportunities, and most problems are best solved in the right kind of collaborative environment. (And if you were to ask the Microsoft employee who looked at the last browser-crash report sent from your laptop, he'd certainly agree—and thank you for your collaboration.)

The design process is a series of conversations that culminate in everyone knowing how and why you got there. So every good organization should have its team primed to understand how far to go and what authorization and signoff they need at every stage of that process.

Home builders come to us and say, "We want to do housing with structural insulated panels because nobody is doing them. They're energy-efficient and they're strong and they're almost soundproof. In fact, they're bulletproof; you can't even penetrate them with a high-velocity semiautomatic round. And we should do basements too!"

These builders believe that uniqueness will be enough to carry their design idea to the market. Unfortunately, some of them are kind of crazy. They've risen to the role of division president in the companies they work for, and because they came from Ohio—where homes have basements—and then moved to California to take over a position for a national home builder, they believe everybody in California wants and needs a basement. Plus, they're in California now and of course people in California like unique things, so structural insulated panels should be a real winner of an idea. So they begin to shop their idea around, and in some cases they will *insist* you do what they're suggesting, even though your professional experience says it is going to be a dismal failure.

There is certainly a place for that attitude if you're a visionary—a genius. And such geniuses of design do exist...guys like Frank Gehry, Frank Lloyd Wright, *et al*.

But Gehry and Wright are outliers, and this is not a book on visionaries. This is a book on how you get things done. And the way you get things done is by having the appropriate balance of input from the right people (and I should emphasize *right*), so that you can understand the value of your work in the eyes of the people who matter most—the ones who are writing the checks.

This respect for others' expertise goes both ways. If you work in the Design Quadrant, you know that your work as a designer isn't finished until the thing you design is built...and you know that a lot can happen to a design in a collaborative process with other experienced professionals.

For example, when I began work on this book, my editor and I put together a book plan—a two-page, chapter-by-chapter summary of what we expected the finished book would look like. That plan was the foundation upon which this book was to be built . . . and by the time we got to this chapter it had been revised at least twice. Why? Because as we worked on the manuscript, we began to realize that certain of its planned parts weren't viable. I also began to think of some other things I wanted to say that weren't accounted for in the original plan.

Then, after I wrote each chapter, my editor would return it covered in red ink: "This paragraph isn't relevant. And this section here would make more sense in Chapter 8." And so on.

I bring this up because it's not uncommon for people in other quadrants to resist changes that need to be made as the design process moves along. Sometimes you'll have a sales manager in your Marketing Quadrant who's a bully (or maybe just an egomaniac), and he'll insist that the work he did in the early stages of the project absolutely must stay—regardless of whether it fits the current iteration of the product. I trust I don't need to explain why that attitude is unproductive.

DESIGN DONE RIGHT

Southwest Airlines is a good example of design done well, with a clear sense of purpose and brand identity. Now, Southwest certainly isn't a luxury carrier—the airline set the bar very low, and rarely disappoints—but it is very, *very* clear about who it is from a design and branding standpoint. "This is what you will get from us: You will more than likely get to your destination on time. You will get a drink and a bag of nuts—or pretzels, if you have a nut allergy—and a flight attendant who is pleasant and concerned about your safety. You can also bring two checked bags at no charge. We guarantee that much . . . but that's it."

That's a really low bar—but Southwest always clears it. Southwest positions itself as a no-frills air-travel option, but what little it does promise, it always delivers. Contrast that with the "full-service" carriers, whose motto, I believe, is "We're not happy until you're not happy." How many organizations can you think of that follow this Front Stage approach to winning your business? Bureaucratic organizations that think they're too big to fail tend to make those kinds of mistakes.

What does all this have to do with design? When Southwest decided what kind of carrier it wanted to be—that is, when it settled on the quality of purpose—the airline designed its approach carefully so that it would always, unfailingly deliver on that promise.

Southwest landed on that formula about fifty years ago, and the company looked in some unusual places for inspiration. It looked to NASCAR, noticing how fast drivers' pit crews could complete a pit stop; the idea was to see how quickly a crew could turn an airplane around after landing and have it ready for takeoff again, because the carrier doesn't make money when the plane is on the ground. Southwest put systems in place that allow it to get jets in the air as quickly as possible. It got the whole staff—both Front Stage and Back Stage people—to pitch in. That means a captain with thirty years of professional experience as a pilot will walk the aisle and pick up newspapers and empty cups in between flights.

Southwest's promise to the public is this: We don't do much, but everything we do had better be pretty doggone good, because this is what we've committed to. And we don't disappoint.

The airline did its homework. It said, "This is how we're going to distinguish ourselves, because this is what we think people want. This is how we can deliver those services and this is how we're going to pitch it." That's attention to design in all areas: in terms of branding, Southwest's processes and procedures align with how it presents itself to the public. In terms of the Q in the Q^3 Quad Mod, it's getting good-quality people, like that captain who picks up newspapers and pretzel wrappers in the aisles because he's bought into the company's culture. And above all, it has paid attention to design in terms of processes for turning the planes around and keeping as many of them in the air as possible at all times.

The result of all this attention to design? Southwest carries more domestic passengers than any other US airline, and according to the Department of Transportation, it receives fewer customer complaints than any other US airline.

We have a saying in our office: "Practice safe design—always use a concept." The concept—the big idea—is the cornerstone of what you do in the Design Quadrant. The Southwest example is so strong because the concept is so simple and strong, and if you can understand the concept that drives your organization, that understanding will inform your work in the Design and Marketing Quadrants.

The strength of the concept, whether you are designing widgets or designing a company, is the metric by which everything else is judged.

CHAPTER 6

THE PRODUCTION QUADRANT

@gapingvoid

NO PRODUCER LIVES IN A VACUUM but is part of a complex system involving all sorts of movings parts.

- Hugh MacLeod

THE NUTS AND BOLTS QUADRANT

The Production Quadrant is where the rubber meets the road—where the actual nuts-and-bolts work of making your product or providing your service actually gets done.

Unfortunately, and despite its obvious importance, the Production Quadrant sometimes doesn't get a lot of respect because it's deep in the dark bowels of the organization's Back Stage. It's a black box—people outside of the organization are generally not encouraged to go back there, and production people, in turn, are not often invited up onto the Front Stage.

I think production people in some organizations sometimes believe they're governed by what might be called "mushroom management": we'll keep you in the dark and pile on the manure, and someday, if you survive, maybe you'll grow tall enough to join us in the sunlight.

That's a mistake, because validating that group and giving it the proper respect can bring incalculable benefits to your organization. Moreover, as I hope I've impressed upon you by now, the Q^3 Quad Mod requires a certain amount of connective tissue between the Front and Back Stages.

BRINGING THE PRODUCTION TEAM IN FROM THE COLD

As I've suggested in previous chapters, in any organization in which there's a lack of mutual respect between the Front and Back Stages, the Back Stage tends to feel it more keenly— they're the mushrooms I alluded to above. And between the two Back Stage quadrants, the problem is more acute in production. Operations teams don't exist completely in a black hole—they can't, because they generate things that directly and immediately affect the other quadrants: reports, reviews, analysis, etc. If you work in the payroll department, you know that narcissist in sales can't ignore your emails—not if he wants to get paid!

But the Production Quadrant, in an organization modeled on the traditional org chart, can easily become an island . . . inhabited, for all you know, by giant gorillas and dinosaurs, ancient tribes of Amazon warriors, or who knows what.

One of the most valuable epiphanies I ever had, from leading my company and from watching how other organizations did things, was that a little bit of love and direct communication go a long way. In addition to the "Behind the Build" practice I described in Chapter 4, we also do a quarterly studio update meeting: every three months we go off-site for a couple of hours and have a nice meal, and I talk about where things are and how they're going, generally. I talk about the culture and the bigger picture, and then my fellow principals talk about some of the details of specific projects. Afterward, we do an anonymous survey, from which we always learn some surprising things about what's important to our team at the moment (as opposed to what I thought was important), and what they want to hear us discuss at the next meeting. We've been doing this for about two years now, and we've found it to be an invaluable tool for keeping the lines between the quadrants nice and blurry. (More on that in a bit.)

The overarching lesson to be learned from this is that what people help to create, they'll support. By involving the entire team in these meetings, we prevent the Production Quadrant from becoming an island. Participation in these kinds of conversations brings the production people out of the Back Stage in a way that they especially need, maybe a bit more than the rest of the team. Designers and marketing people? They're talking all the time. They're reviewing one another's work and collaborating constantly, both across and within quadrants. Production doesn't get that much of an opportunity, so the way we've been able infuse our culture into the production team is via the quarterly studio update meeting.

We have also invited production team members to be part of the design review. When we go from design to production, a lot of things need to happen, not just in our architectural firm, but in every organization: the design team comes up with an idea, and then the production team needs to be galvanized so the idea can be brought to life—so that it can become real. That's what the production team does, and when they have benefit of hearing what the designers' challenges were, they're much better equipped to enthusiastically embrace the challenge of producing what has been designed.

They also want to have a voice, to have their expert opinions heard in the matter of *what* they'll be producing. That's why we do hand-off meetings when the project moves from design to production. Then, at key milestones of the project, we reconvene the design and production teams for what we call pin-ups, where we pin the progress up on the wall and review it for consistency with the vision.

BLURRY LINES

Most of our clients are builders. They have their own Front and Back Stages within their organizations, and they have to build what we design: we produce documents, and from those documents, they have to produce homes and buildings. But they don't have the same expertise we have when it comes to producing those documents they work from.

So on occasion, we'll bring along someone from our Production Quadrant to a client meeting—both because it helps us to communicate what we're trying to do, and because, as I said before, we've found that what people help to create, they'll support.

Now, let's say that during one of these meetings, we explain that we want to do a NanaWall in a building, which is basically a sliding glass wall that disappears from the rim and completely opens up the space. The purchasing agent or the general contractor may balk and say, "That is absolutely not in the budget!"

OK, we'll say—and then we turn to our production person and ask, "What could we do that would accomplish the same thing?" And he may reply, "Well, maybe we can't do a NanaWall, but I sourced this new product that is a lot cheaper than the NanaWall and looks almost as good, and I think it'll do the same thing. And it's half the price." That kind of collaboration—esteeming and involving the production team at the right time, in the right place, with the right mindset—can benefit all the stakeholders. People feel a little more empowered in their jobs, and we get the benefit of their expertise at an important moment when we might otherwise not have had it.

I've seen other companies use this strategy to great effect, and I've seen great discoveries emerge from the serendipitous synchronicity that can result. I once attended a conference where a high-end appliance manufacturer decided to bring a mockup of a new product that was still in development. It couldn't be made out of stainless steel because it wasn't in production, so the mockups were constructed from metalized plastic that looked like charcoal-colored stainless steel—and everybody went bananas for this material. The manufacturer was completely unprepared for it.

Fortunately, the manufacturer had brought research and development people along to this conference, so these Back Stage team members had a chance to see how excited the market got over the color and the material of the mockup—as opposed to the placement of the knobs, for example. They went back and figured out how to create a production-quality material that emulated the look.

That's a good example of what can happen when you open the curtain into the Back Stage a little, and then bring those Back Stage people—the *right* Back Stage people, as I'll explain shortly—forward so that they can see what can happen. And since they were right there to observe people's reactions to this material, they weren't so quick to say, "Well, no, we can't do that. That's not possible." All they could do was sit there and listen . . . and after hearing this response from every architect, designer, and builder who came through there, they said, "OK, we need to figure this out, because clearly, people love it."

When you have a new product, you need to try to create these blurry lines between quadrants, because production, sales and marketing, and design will all need to be involved in bringing this new thing to market. Involving the Back Stage in sales meetings can give your sales team confidence: *The brainiacs who work in the back room don't know how to sell things, but if they can show us that this works, we will believe them.* So the thing that production people bring to the organization on the Front Stage, more than anything else, is credibility. Because when those production people, say, "Yes, this is possible—we can do this," it has tremendous credibility with the market.

WHEN DO YOU OPEN YOUR KIMONO? (AND WHO IS HIDDEN BEHIND IT?)

One huge value opportunity in business is being purposeful about when you open your kimono—that is, exactly when and how you allow people to see the inner workings behind the curtain in the Production Quadrant. As I said in Chapter 3, *time and place* are of utmost importance. There's a time and a place to discuss things with the production team in the Back Stage, and there's a time and place to bring those production people into a Front Stage discussion. One benefit of doing this is that your clientele will believe they're getting a peek behind the curtain, which of course is exciting and empowering for them.

But it has to be done at the right time . . . and perhaps more important, it has to be *the right people.* As I've noted elsewhere in this book, a lot of Back Stage people end up on the Back Stage because that's where they're comfortable. They're creative or administrative people by nature, and many of them are ill at ease in the spotlight. But if you're going to put someone there, in front of the curtain, they need to be able to overcome that reticence.

Further, your Back Stage people on the Front Stage need to understand how Front Stage activities work. They need to understand that salespeople will sometimes make what may seem like outlandish promises, which can then be walked back toward what's actually feasible. And while this is going on, your Back Stage people on the Front Stage need to be able to keep their cool and tell their faces not to show their discomfort.

When you're on the Front Stage with Back Stage team members, those Back Stage people need to trust their Front Stage colleagues implicitly. It's kind of like when pilots do aerobatics. A pilot might have thousands of flight hours under his belt; he might even be a professional pilot . . . but he's never done aerobatics before. So he'll go on a flight with a highly qualified aerobatic instructor and get completely freaked out because it's not an area that he has any experience with. He's been flying for maybe his whole life, but he's never been upside down! My friends who are aerobatic instructors will tell me that the worst people to take on an aerobatic ride are pilots, because they're uncomfortable not knowing what to expect next.

And people in the Production Quadrant can suffer from that.

A number of years ago, Sean and I were on our way into a client meeting, and we had with us some color boards—a lot of them. In a situation like this, you have fifteen of them for three new model homes with three different elevation styles and two or three color palettes. There's a lot of colors, right? And you have to think about how they're going to go together. You have to think about the psychology behind color, whether accent colors should go in certain places on the building, etc. It's a science, and today we have a colorist on staff, and all that person does is pick out colors for buildings, believe it or not. It's a full-time job.

This was before we had a colorist, however. We're architects and designers, so color is very integral to what we do—some colors go better with certain styles than others. The team came up with the color schemes, and Sean, who was the project manager at the time, went with me to present these colors to the client, carrying these twenty-four-by-thirty-six-inch boards with samples on them.

Just before we went inside we got to a sunny spot on the sidewalk near the front door, and I stopped Sean and held out one of the boards and said, "What color is this?" And he told me. And I said, "OK, what color is *this* one?" And he told me. "This is green, and this is bluish-green, and then this is kind of a royal blue."

"OK," I said. "Great." We went inside and had a very productive meeting with the client. We presented our colors, and the client loved them. After the meeting, the moment we walked outside, Sean turned to me and said, "What was that business in the sunlight all about before we went in there?"

"Oh, I said, I'm colorblind."

A lot of people would have been freaked out—Sean didn't know that I was colorblind when we walked in there. But, being a Front Stage person, he adapted to the curveball I threw him because *he trusted me*. And likewise, when you bring a production person with you to a sales meeting, a conference, or any other Front Stage environment, they need to trust you just as deeply.

This is the potential danger Back Stage people face in Front Stage environments. If your sales manager begins to improvise, or if she makes a deadline promise that sounds tight, your production guy can't flip out and sandbag that promise. He has to keep a poker face.

If you're an entrepreneur, you probably spend most of your time on the Front Stage. That's your role, your place—but you need to know who your Back Stage people are, what their strengths are, and recognize that the difference between your strengths and theirs doesn't make them lesser. They're just different people, with different strengths, a different focus, and different roles that need to be respected.

Again, some Back Stage folks are uncomfortable in the spotlight—they're not gregarious by nature, and that can manifest in a meeting in a number of ways: They can clam up and just go completely silent. Or they can actually act disrespectful, because they don't know how not to do that. Or they might not respect the sales manager's ability to do improv, which they may see as disingenuous.

That's not the person you want to bring up front.

The area of your business with the biggest potential to enable you to disrupt an industry is probably the Production Quadrant. Understanding it, understanding its influence on the Front Stage, and understanding the richness of ideas that you can mine from it: there lies your greatest opportunity.

It's what Uber did. Uber was a great idea, but the idea doesn't work without the platform . . . and it was production people who built that platform.

Jeff Bezos once boasted that he could fill up a whiteboard with a hundred ideas in an hour.[1] But the brilliance doesn't lie in the idea. It lies in the ability to produce the idea, to execute it. There are countless good ideas out there, but you can't make them real without production.

When I was thinking about being an architect at the ripe old age of about fifteen or sixteen, my dad told me, "You need to work out in the field. You need to see how things are built, and it'll make you a better architect." Our lead designer here, the principal in charge of design at our firm—*he* worked out in the field. He actually knows how to build stuff, and the best designers that I know are the ones who know how things go together. They know how to produce things. And so, where disruption is concerned . . . you disrupt because you know *how things work*, not because you just want to act on some goofy-assed idea that you threw out there. There are plenty of those out there already.

Your idea has got to be actionable, and that's what production does. They make it real.

CHAPTER 7

THE OPERATIONS QUADRANT

operations
silos
are the
kiss of
death

@gapingvoid

PEOPLE LOVE THEIR SILOS. Like a good Irish bar, they're safe, they're familiar, they're comfy, they're where your friends hang out, they're where everything is where it should be. But they're also dangerous, because they cut you off from reality. And reality is what will kill you when you're not looking and also where all the real future opportunities are.

- Hugh MacLeod

THE FIRST RUNG OF THE LADDER

Some things are universal. It doesn't matter whether you're a design professional, a manufacturer, or a law firm; it doesn't matter *what* kind of company you are—there are some givens in every business.

You need a business license. If you have employees, you need insurance. You need an HR manual (it's required in a lot of states). You have to have all your ducks in a row with various local, state, and federal agencies—they need to know you exist so they can tax you. If you are dealing with independent contractors, you need to know how to insure them.

Apart from the various legal and tax requirements listed above, there are other day-to-day necessities to consider: you have to keep your payroll running smoothly. Invoices need to go out, collections need to be handled, cost and revenue projections need to be made, and so on.

Far from the public face of your organization, hidden from the clients' view, the people in your Operations Quadrant are taking care of all these things. They toil endlessly at an endless series of what, to some, may seem like mundane tasks, each less glamorous and less sexy than the one before it—and every one of them absolutely vital to your survival. While some people may find these functions dull or tedious, there are others whose gift is the skills to handle these tasks—and for them, the work is fun and exciting. Things that I don't get excited about? There's someone out there who does. That's the essence of right person + right role + right fit = profound energy in the organization!

This is where the credibility of a company is forged. An Operations Quadrant is what distinguishes an *organization* from a business run by a self-employed contractor. Having an Operations Quadrant is the first rung on the ladder of business legitimacy—after all, if you're self-employed, you don't have to do any of this stuff. You're not working out of your mom's basement anymore. You're going to have leases to deal with. You're going to have realtors to deal with. Countless legal, financial, and tax obligations are handled by this quadrant.

A lot of entrepreneurs, because they're so vision-oriented, either take this for granted or assume that at the end of the year they can just pull a few things together and everything that needs to happen *will* happen—magically. But if you're a small, growing business, the Operations Quadrant is probably the easiest place to get into trouble, because you're liable to be lax about the three components of your operation that are the easiest to neglect: money in, money out, and taxes.

If you don't handle those three things well—and a lot of new businesses don't handle them well—you will not be in business very long. If you always cobble things together at the last minute ("Oh, my gosh! It's the end of the month. It's the end of the quarter. We need to get our bills together!"), you will fail to capture all the value you've created for your clients or customers. You will be leaving money on the table. People will be getting things that they didn't pay for. You will not be nearly as successful as you should be, and you will be frustrated.

And for vision-oriented entrepreneurs, taking these things for granted is really, really easy to do.

Operations can bring value to your entire organization. It's the fulcrum of the seesaw, the hinge point on which everything else balances. That's how important it is—and that's why not getting it right is a huge problem.

THE ISLAND QUADRANT

A job in the Operations Quadrant, more than in any other part of an organization, is the quintessential Back Stage position. The Operations Quadrant is distinct from the rest of the organization in that it doesn't connect to the other quadrants as easily and naturally as they all do to one another. As we've seen in previous chapters, the Design Quadrant in particular has close relationships with the Marketing and Production Quadrants, and there is a lot of overlap in their responsibilities and spheres of influence.

But operations is isolated. There is minimal Venn-diagram overlap between its responsibilities and those of the other quadrants. An invisible barrier seems to separate operations from everyone else. While much of this separation is by necessity due to confidentiality requirements of HR, insurance, salaries, client information, etc., there are ways to integrate with the rest of the team while maintaining discretion.

Now, it may be necessary in some organizations to maintain some semblance of that barrier to prevent operations from acquiring too much weight relative to the other quadrants (more on that in a bit). But the barrier, if it's permitted to stand, must always be permeable so that clear communication is always possible, and so that the Operations Quadrant is subject to the same due scrutiny as the others.

MY OWN EXPERIENCES WITH OPERATIONS

Some years ago we had a manager within our organization who oversaw this stuff, and that person led me to believe he was doing a really good job . . . until I realized he wasn't.

It took me a long time to realize this, partly because we're a relatively good-sized organization, and partly because . . . well, my dad had a saying: "Money is no big deal as long as you have enough of it." And we had enough. We were doing OK, delivering our services, and we had good cash flow. So I figured things must be good. If you're the entrepreneur who's in charge of vision and responsible for most of the things that happen on the Front Stage, you have to trust that your colleague—your leader in operations—is doing a good job on the Back Stage.

But as Warren Buffett said, you'll know who's been swimming without a bathing suit when the tide goes out. Well, in 2008 the tide went out, and suddenly we could see that a whole bunch of swimmers in the Operations Quadrant didn't have bathing suits. It was shocking.

It's fairly easy to get complacent when you're doing well and resources are abundant. But when the Great Recession hit, it was clear that the Operations Quadrant had been coasting along, trusting that collections would take care of themselves and that workflow and resources were being managed. When the faucet of work was turned off, they started dipping into our credit line and using up savings rather than putting strong processes in place to handle the fundamentals and keep the business healthy.

As the leader of the organization at a time like this, you have to take responsibility for these kinds of problems, and then you've got to lead the solution. So, after we weathered the recession, we moved that person up a rung—in addition to overseeing production, he would now handle the Operations Quadrant in the position of CFO.

More problems arose, however, when this leader built his own silo and secluded himself in it. Operations became insulated from the rest of the organization . . . and from me.

This person was a living example of the Peter Principle in action—the idea that people are eventually elevated to the level of their incompetence. Unfortunately, that incompetence isn't usually discovered until something traumatic happens—say, a recession hits, or you get audited, or you want to increase your line of credit and you have to provide financials—and all of a sudden you see things that you didn't see before because those reports are now being shown to you in a different way. (You never see things as clearly as when you're looking through someone else's eyes.)

If someone told me five years ago that I, a creative architect and designer, would be spending significant focus and creativity in the Back Stage area, and specifically in operations, I'd have said they were nuts. But at the end of 2015, the operations team and I met with our outside CPA to get a good look at where we were at year-end. I walked into that meeting thinking, *Let's get some cash out of the company and pay bonuses.*

But there was limited cash. A report showed that our accounts receivable were not doing well.

The problem wasn't that we weren't busy; we had work on the books. We were meeting our clients' goals . . . but we weren't meeting our own business goals. The money wasn't being collected consistently, and there was no process for billing, collections, etc. Everything was being done in an ad hoc way from month to month. Our CFO was just grabbing the low-hanging fruit. Contracts were not getting done in a timely manner. He wasn't responding to communications from his team in a timely manner.

But he would always tell me what he thought I wanted to hear—I later learned that his subordinates were often instructed, "Don't tell Jeff any bad news"—so these failures went undetected for a long time.

On top of that, this Back Stage leader was taking on Front Stage tasks he wasn't suited for.

To a lot of people, contract negotiation seems like a Front Stage activity—after all, you're dealing with people outside your organization. But in a lot of organizations, the legal or accounting departments end up getting deeply involved in contract negotiations because these often have legal implications. In our field, however, the terms and conditions of most contracts are pretty much generally accepted industry standards. Nevertheless, this individual tended to introduce unnecessary complications. Why? I can't say for sure, but I suspect that he had a need to be validated, to feel important in the organization.

When people are taking something simple and making it hard or complex just for the sake of trying to prove their value, that's a red flag you should really pay attention to. "Why is this such a hard question? Why is it taking so long?" If you're on the Front Stage and you're wondering that, you need to pay attention to that intuition.

If you've got operations people negotiating contracts, you need to remember that they're not really Front Stage people. If you're a Front Stage person working in sales, marketing, or design, you have a passion for your work, and you know that you need to get things done in a certain way, on a certain schedule.

But operations, under a traditional org-chart model, has a slightly different sense of urgency. The person who was overseeing our contracts acted like a gatekeeper, always coming up with reasons why things couldn't be done, rather than figuring out how things *could* be done. We had the wrong person in the job—he was a talented guy in many respects, but he should not have been doing contracts. He had the legal and business mind for the task, but he didn't have that sense of urgency that Front Stage people do, and he didn't perform well on the Front Stage.

The Operations Quadrant of our organization was becoming too heavy, acquiring too much weight relative to the other quadrants, and—dare I say it—getting too bureaucratic! (Which is essentially a four-letter word in my world.) Worse, they were taking on the wrong *kind* of weight. They were flexing their muscles in other quadrants in a way we didn't want, while still holding on to a siloed mentality that inhibited communication and coordination with those quadrants. It was a culture problem that permeated the quadrant.

The funny thing about weight: people who are taking on extra weight—extra responsibilities—will believe they're important. They see it as a positive thing, but in reality it's an anchor. Remember the mobile analogy from Chapter 2? People carrying an inappropriate workload, involving themselves in activities that aren't (or shouldn't be) within the scope of their duties or skillset, are like bricks hanging from a mobile above a baby's crib. They're pulling everything down, making it impossible for the Q^3 Quad Mod to balance on its axis and float. When the model is unbalanced, when one quadrant has too much weight, the thing is going to fall off of its axis—and that's what happened to us.

That meeting with our CPA and the financial team in 2015 was a big epiphany for me; it was then that I realized the real disconnect between operations and the rest of the organization: operations had built an impenetrable silo, and it was negatively affecting me and the rest of the team, hindering our ability to succeed.

So I spent the next three months looking through all our documents—articles of incorporation, how we were structured as an organization, etc. And in January of 2016, I took the keys to the car—the organization being the car—away from him and I put the keys in the ignition and turned it on. The gas tank was on empty. I looked in the glove box and found a bunch of fuel vouchers all crumpled up and just stuffed in there (i.e., the collections backlog). I spent about a month and a half carefully organizing and following up on all these vouchers, and I discovered we were doing a lot better than the person in charge of operations had led me and others to believe. It was appalling: that person had created such a fiefdom in his little silo that he was beginning to tell people in the organization—and some people outside the organization—that we were insolvent!

I spent three months, sixteen hours a day, six days a week, on the Front Stage, on the Back Stage, and in the micrograin of our organization; I was committed to making things work in a proper way. I immediately began to put some things in place. I made myself directly accessible to the financial director of our organization. I needed to get the most traction in the least amount of time, so I looked carefully at all our contracts. Within two days, I'd filled up a couple of whiteboards and found six months' worth of stray revenue: contracts that weren't being followed up on, contracts for additional services that weren't being written, deals that weren't being closed—all the responsibilities of the person in the Operations Quadrant. All this time he'd been telling me I just needed to go out and market more because there wasn't enough business. What I did, essentially, was stack the dirty dishes. It was like when the dishwasher comes in at five to an overflowing sink of dishes because everyone has been just tossing everything in there. The first thing a smart dishwasher—a professional dishwasher—will do is take a half-hour and sort things out. Now you know what you've got to deal with and you can efficiently and effectively tackle the task.

The next thing I did was look at the reports the project managers were being given, and the information they were populating the reports with. I asked someone in the financial department, "Why are the dollar amounts not represented in the reports?"

His response was, "Well, the person in charge of operations doesn't want the project managers to see." It turned out that the person in charge of operations was concerned that if the project managers knew how much was on there, they would start to feel too good about how much influence they had in the organization.

I said, "So . . . any project might be a $20,000 project or a $500,000 project. How do the project managers know how to resource the project or to set up a proper deadline? How do they know how to budget?"

The answer was, "Well, they need to go and ask the person in charge of operations."

I'll pause my narrative here to let you absorb that until your head starts to hurt.

I said, "OK, that's gonna change. How much trouble is it going to be for you to be able to show the numbers?"

He said, "Just give me a minute, Jeff. I'll be right back." He came back in two minutes and said, "Here you go."

I asked him, "How did you get all the numbers so quickly?" He said, "Oh, they are on reports. I just don't print them with that column exposed because I was told not to."

I said OK, that changes right now. And at the next meeting, we presented the new reports with all the numbers on them.

In January of 2016 I created a different future for the person who had made such a mess of my Operations Quadrant—a future not in my organization. Reading this, you're no doubt thinking, *Why would you put up with this? How could this have happened?* The bottom-line reason was that we had a long history together and I trusted him—an entrepreneur *should* be able to trust his colleagues.

I wasn't completely unaware of his shortcomings. I had spent years trying to develop and evolve him, practically begging him, "*Please* do something to enrich yourself. Take a class, a seminar, spend some time with a peer—*something.* Anything." It's painful to see someone who is actively committed to not changing. If the people close to you in your organization don't want to be challenged and don't want to grow, then you have to grow without them. And when they begin to become an anchor and hold you back, then they need to go.

Astute readers will notice that I had all these problems with this partner in 2015—five years after my Q^3 epiphany at PDX airport. Why did these kinds of problems persist so long after I'd conceived the Q^3 Quad Mod?

The answer is that there's a difference between having the model and living it. We were employing the model, but we weren't fully exploiting it. Also, the concept of the model, by itself, isn't enough. You need processes to support business activities within the quadrants.

Not rules—but *processes*.

RELIGION VS. SPIRITUALITY—AND RULES VS. PRINCIPLES AND PROCESSES

I've been part of organizations that were way too operations-heavy from a rules and regulation standpoint, and it puts me in mind of the difference between religion and spirituality. People sometimes ask me if I'm religious, and I tell them no. I do not like religion—but I am absolutely spiritual.

What's the difference? Well, religion is all about the rules—a whole bunch of rules to follow . . . and guess what? Nobody can really follow them. Spirituality, by contrast, is about having a relationship with something outside of yourself that you believe in, and that relationship is just like any other relationship: you have great conversations, you help others, and you are helped in turn. That's what spirituality is.

The difference between an entrepreneurial organization and a bureaucratic organization can be expressed in the same terms. You want to have relationships—with your team members and with your clients. And you want processes, but you don't want *rules*. Once you have rules, then people will find ways to circumvent the rules. If you have principles and processes, however, then people begin to realize they are working toward something together.

The people who work in the Operations Quadrant, from the accounting and legal departments to HR, are often seen as the rule keepers: "Your timesheet is not in yet. Turn it in by 5:00 p.m. or you won't be paid this week! We have one month a year when you can change your insurance, and if you don't get it done during that window of time, you're screwed!"

There also seem to be a lot of rules foisted on entrepreneurial organizations by state, local, and federal government bureaucracies. We need to do a lot of reporting as a result—and a lot can go awry if we get that reporting wrong. I finally dealt with this problem four years ago, and we now have an HR manager—which is kind of a luxury for a firm our size. We have this amazing woman who is the missing link, if you will, between operations and the other quadrants. She speaks operations, and she understands the rules. I sometimes tell her, "I don't need an HR manager to tell me all the things I *can't* do. I need an HR manager to help me do the things that I want to do and not get sued."

She never goes to lunch alone. She always takes a team member with her—or a couple of team members— just to check in with them. To ask them, "How's it going?" To assess their cultural alignment with our organization. She's always meeting with people, checking in with people. I like that, because we get feedback that way, and dialogue is important to a healthy organization.

My organization and I had a problem with an operations leader who, among his other shortcomings, had a tendency to

CHAPTER 8

LIGHTNING BOLT LEADERSHIP:
IN CHARGE, NOT IN CONTROL

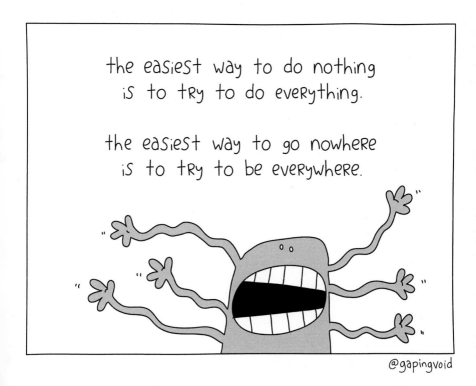

TO TRY AND DO EVERYTHING IS AS POINTLESS AS TRYING TO BE EVERYBODY. There's just you, so just be you, and be the best you ever.

- Hugh MacLeod

BE A LIGHTNING BOLT, NOT A CONTROL FREAK

In earlier chapters we discussed the importance of everyone understanding their proper role in an organization . . . and that includes you, the leader.

Nobody wants to work for a control freak, and because these days it's the norm for someone to work for many different companies in the course of a career (often as an independent contractor), nobody *has* to work for one.

This is a chapter about the distinction between being in charge and being in control . . . and about being in charge without being in control. It can be terrifying for an entrepreneur to give up control, but if you learn the distinction between those two concepts, you will reap enormous rewards. I envision a cloud floating above the Q^3 Quad Mod, which is the place where vision lives. It is your job to live in that cloud and toss lightning bolts into the Q^3 Quad Mod and create great energy for the team, not to micromanage.

LONE WOLVES

In Chapter 1, I mentioned a certain type of entrepreneur, the lone wolf, whose business can't survive without his unflagging, ceaseless devotion. Lone wolves' very identity is completely wrapped up in their business, and in themselves as the titular head of that business—so, as a result, if the lone wolf is not there, then the business doesn't do well.

Being a lone-wolf entrepreneur is extremely limiting. It will only take you so far because it's tied, essentially, to how much you can build or how much you can generate with a team of five to twelve people. Moreover, you can't achieve any kind of freedom in your life when you're chained to your business. The term *lone wolf* may conjure a romantic image of a trailblazing maverick, unbeholden to any pack . . . but the truth is that a lone-wolf entrepreneur is less free than any of the members of the team, with a whole lot more risk and responsibility.

I have friends who are architects, people I've known since we were in college together. When I went to my class reunion a few years ago, the ones who had their own practices were shocked by my success. We're all about the same age, obviously, but none of them had achieved anywhere near the level of prosperity I had. They were convinced I had to be doing something untoward—no architect could be that successful! They would grow their businesses for a while and get to fifteen people, and then they'd go back down to twelve, then down to ten, because they hit what Dan Sullivan calls the *ceiling of complexity*—the point at which a company cannot grow any further by using its existing knowledge and skill sets.[1]

The ceiling of complexity is a particular problem for lone wolves. As they grow, from a one-person operation to a small company working out of a home office, to a bigger company renting a small office, to a huge firm that takes up an entire floor of a building, they have trouble letting go of the responsibilities they used to have.

Dan is fond of saying, "The skills that got you out of Egypt are not the skills that will get you to the promised land." As leaders and as managers, the demands that we have to put on ourselves and the people we lead will inevitably grow as we become more successful, and at some point every entrepreneur must face the reality that, thanks to his own efforts, his job has outgrown him.

INSPIRATION

An entrepreneur is typically somewhat of a generalist, even within fields of high specialization like software design. That is to say, if you're an entrepreneur, there are likely several things you're good at.

But not all of the things you *can* do—even the ones you're good at—are necessarily things you *should* be doing. Your job is to receive and act upon *inspiration*. Your job— and in all likelihood, the very reason you became an entrepreneur in the first place—is to have great ideas and bring them into the world. To take the lightning bolts issuing from your brain and cast them into the marketplace, like Zeus hurling lightning bolts down from Mount Olympus. Your job is to imagine a better way to build the proverbial mousetrap, and to inspire investors and employees to work with you to make it happen. To take something of low value and make it highly valuable.

Your job, in short, is to be a leader.

Inspiration, as a concept, is important in other ways as well—you also need to inspire your team, and to be the kind of leader who can inspire them. That may sound self-evident, but the leaders of strong, fast-growing organizations often lose sight of that central truth about their role, and this can make them prone to the antithesis of leadership—micromanagement.

Most entrepreneurs, whether they're lifelong lone wolves or lone wolves who've begun to find themselves leading larger and larger packs, have this mindset that everything that happens within the organization is their responsibility.

It's hard to reach the point in your growth trajectory where you can no longer keep your finger on every button of the machine you've built. It's hard to bring yourself to give up that control. But you *have* to give it up—even if the people you delegate to sometimes make mistakes . . . because people need to make mistakes. If you bully or coddle your team into letting you do everything for them—work that you are *paying them* to do—then they will never feel empowered to fully actualize their potential so the organization can benefit from their talent.

The way you look at problems defines you as a leader. During my second year in business we had someone working for us as Director of First Impressions (i.e., the receptionist). It was essentially an entry-level position, but we like to give people the opportunity to grow, so she was assigned a task that, in hindsight, may have been a little above her pay grade—and then left her to her own devices. And she made a gigantic mistake that cost the organization $50,000.

What happened? She mixed up the numbers on a couple of projects; both were the same type of project, but one of them was much more expensive than the other. She sent the lower number to the client who should have had the higher number, and vice-versa. The client who got the lower number went, "*Woo-hoo*, this is great! we expected it to be $50,000 more!" And the client who got the other contract called us and shouted, "Why are you guys gouging me? This was supposed to be $50,000 less!"

Untangling that mess was a big, expensive headache, and we had to eat the difference on the higher-dollar project. When this was brought to my attention, I looked at it and meditated on it for a couple of minutes, and then I asked her to come into my office. She was, obviously, quite upset. I said, "Can you tell me what happened?" And she told me.

"OK, I said, "this is how I look at the situation. This has cost us $50,000—and it is part of your education."

Looking at me in terror and disbelief, she asked, "Are you going to fire me?"

I said, "No, I just made a $50,000 investment in you. The stupidest thing I could do would be to fire you. Do you think you will ever make that mistake again?"

"No," she said, "I will never make that mistake again." And she never did. Not only that, but she told the story to other people in the organization.

And it makes me proud that she did that. Again, I didn't do it for any other reason except that, as I saw it, I'd just invested $50,000 in this person—and maybe other people as well, if her example could save them from making the same kind of mistake.

I told her, "I don't like the fact that this mistake just cost us a lot of money . . . but I do like the fact that you have the right heart, that you're not being defensive, that you're taking responsibility for this. Why would I want to get rid of you? I love you. Thank you. Don't do it again. Be creative enough to make a new mistake—just maybe see if it could cost less the next time!"

I got caught in the trap of the lone wolf myself when I was a younger entrepreneur, but I learned it's vital to get past the mentality that *nobody can do it as well as me and you didn't do it the same way that I would have done it.* You can never grow as an entrepreneur if you are stuck in that mindset.

I used to work fourteen hours a day. I'd be at the office at 4:30 or 5:00 a.m. most mornings, and I usually would get home around 8:00 at night. And I did that for several years. I used to work on all the designs and present them with a couple of other people on the team. I used to do all the client interaction. I used to review the construction documents—and I did a really bad job before I finally delegated that task; that was my first delegation.

One day a business partner of mine said, "There is this workshop that I go to quarterly, and you should really go."

"I don't have time," I said.

"That's probably the biggest reason why you should go," he said. "Because you don't have extra time for anything. You have zero margin in your life."

I wasn't having a lot of fun in those days. Yes, the insane hours I was putting in and the overextension of my attention capacity were gratifying from a business standpoint.

My ego was well fed because clients were relying on me, and my team was relying on me. I was a very important guy. But I was a legend in my own mind. I was burning myself out and making myself less effective.

And so I bit the bullet and went to this workshop, which is called Strategic Coach—and I would highly recommend it to any entrepreneurs who want more out of their business and life. A lot of the principles in this book I learned or have developed as a result of my participation in Strategic Coach.

The first exercise we were asked to do was absolutely life changing. We did an activity inventory, listing all the things we do in a given week. I filled out the grid pad, and there were 113 things that I did on a weekly basis—everything from reviewing every invoice and opening the mail to having conversations with clients, negotiating contracts, writing contracts, establishing scope and fees for all the contracts, and coming up with new designs.

The next thing you did was circle the tasks at which you are incompetent. Then you circled the things you are fair at. Then the things you excel at. Finally, you circled the things you *love* to do, that you have boundless energy for, and—this is what distinguishes it from a hobby—that people are willing to pay for. And that's what Strategic Coach calls your *Unique Ability*. Every person has one or two, maybe three things they do better than anybody else.

The value of this exercise should be self-evident. What I did—and it wasn't an overnight process—was start at the bottom and begin to delegate the things I was incompetent at. I didn't like them, I didn't get good results, and nobody was going to pay me a dime to do them—they were just things I'd always believed I had to do, so I'd always done them. But no more.

Then I looked at the things I was reasonably competent at, but that someone else could do better, and I gave those up willingly.

I can scarcely describe the feeling you get from following through on this exercise. It is like giving yourself permission to avoid doing things that drive you nuts. Even if other people expect you to do them, you need to stop: you need to say, "I don't do this. There are other ways I can be of value in our relationship, and I'm going to focus on those."

It took me eighteen months to get to the point where I was really focusing on my Unique Ability. It's a process of constant refinement, focus, and evaluation, and it's been incredibly rewarding and liberating. I'm here to tell you that you become a lot more successful when you begin to approach your life in that way.

As a lone-wolf entrepreneur, you believe it is incumbent upon you to take responsibility for *everything*, because you have done everything before and you've done it at a certain level and you know what to expect from yourself. I felt like I'd been smacked in the head with a two-by-four when one of the young leaders in my organization pointed out that no one would ever be able to do things the way that I did. He asked me, "Do you really want to be here all the time and overseeing and doing *everything*? Or do you want to say, 'These are the standards we are working toward; let's all grow into them together'?"

You have to ask yourself as an entrepreneur: Are you doing this for yourself, or are you doing this for your organization? And is your ego too tied to the work that goes out of here? I began to say, "I lead you in your efforts, but you don't work for me—all of us, including me, work for this organization." And when I did that, everything changed.

We're trying to build a legacy here, and the way we do that is by helping people understand that everyone, including the founder of the organization, works *for the organization*. And that understanding helps entrepreneurs realize that there is something outside themselves that they should be working for and toward.

LEGACY LEADERSHIP

I hope my use of the word legacy in that last paragraph doesn't strike you as grandiloquent. I don't use it lightly— and if you're serious about what you do with your working days, you have to be willing sometimes to see your work in grandiose terms. And you can only take your work as seriously as you need to if you have a passion for it.

You have to be passionate about what you do, and you can't be afraid to share that passion. You need to be purposeful about the way you bring forth the work you do, because people want to be around someone who is lit up by what they do.

And then you've got to be willing to provide direction. That doesn't mean solving problems for people who are paid to solve their own problems; it means providing big-picture direction—getting your team to see your organization the same way you yourself see it.

And that takes a lot of reflection, because there's a right way to do it and a wrong way to do it.

I've mentioned Dan Sullivan twice in this book, and once already in this chapter, but I'll drop him just one more plug here: Sullivan says that all progress starts by telling the truth. I can freely and comfortably articulate these things because throughout the course of my career as a leader and an entrepreneur, I have not always done them right.

You need feedback. You have to be accountable to a peer group that has your best interest at heart—think of them as your advisory committee, an adjunct board of directors, if you will, that you can put together before you grow big enough to have a real board of directors. You need people who will speak in a truthful way that will provide you a safe place to think out loud about the problems and opportunities that exist for you, the entrepreneur.

It takes tremendous emotional intelligence to be a leader, and that emotional intelligence has to be a commitment. That means yes, you can have a bad day—you can have a philosophical impasse (also known as an argument) with your spouse before you leave for the office in the morning. (I mean, that's a fact of life!) But you've got to be able to take that negative energy and say, "Not now." You cannot let it color how you present yourself, because as soon as you walk in and begin to interact with your team, they *know* how you are doing. They know because they are watching you. There are a thousand different ways your body language and your facial expressions can betray what's going on in your head if you're having a bad day. It is reflected on your face, in your skin tone, in how you walk, and in how you carry yourself (I would refer you to Daniel Goleman's book, *Emotional Intelligence*, and Malcolm Gladwell's book, *Blink*, if you want to go deeper on this topic) .

As a leader, you have to act your way into a feeling; you cannot afford the luxury of feeling your way into an action, and that requires a deep commitment to emotional intelligence. It means being aware of yourself and being aware of the most important thing that you have as a leader—your impact. We all have to own our impact; nobody else is responsible for it but us.

This is not a "fake it till you make it" kind of thing. Rather, it's an authentic understanding of the effect your behavior has on the world around you. I have a responsibility to a whole lot of people, and I don't want to mess that up. I don't want my mood to ruin their day. That is the preparation you have to make to get the strongest commitment from your people and the best results from your organization.

THE NECESSITY OF SELF IMPROVEMENT

To be an entrepreneur who is not just a self-employed independent contractor or a lone-wolf entrepreneur, you've got to be committed to lifelong learning and growth. As I said earlier in this chapter, the skills that got you out of Egypt are not the skills that will take you to the promised land. As a leader, as an entrepreneur, and as a manager, you have got to be committed to lifelong learning and self-improvement if you truly want to grow your business into a legacy, because the skills that got you to where you are will not get you to the next level.

Being committed to lifelong growth, to learning and making yourself better first so that you can make others better around you: that's what distinguishes a legacy kind of leader. That's what infuses the energy into the lightning bolt; that's the friction that makes the static electricity happen so the lightning can strike. That static—that friction—isn't always comfortable, because as a leader you have to constantly challenge yourself.

As an entrepreneur, you have to be enough of a rugged individualist to believe in your own ability to step out into the world and get things done. You need to be willing to drink a little from the cup of your own ego. But that elixir becomes a poison when you begin to overindulge—when you get to a certain size and you stop allowing fresh ideas into your mindset.

One more thing about self-improvement: you need to stay healthy. That means a healthy mind, body, and spirit. You have got to take care of yourself. That means regular sleep and exercise, and eating well.

And you've got to be vigilant about the toxic people in your life, and balance their inevitable impact with people who are not energy drainers—the trusted advisory group I mentioned earlier in this chapter. You've got to find people you respect who love you from a business standpoint and believe in you.

These are the people who can recharge your battery.

GRATITUDE FOR THE ELEGANT HEADACHES

It's a badge of honor for a lot of leaders to gripe about their problems. And that's one way to look at the world. But another way to look at it is to see problems as opportunities to change things for the better. How we make things better, and how we respond to our opportunities, reflect on the quality of our businesses.

The quality of our problems reflects the quality of our lives. Often the problems we think we have are really what I call *Elegant Headaches*.

What's an Elegant Headache? It's similar to what is now fashionably called a "first-world problem"—that is, any complaint that is clearly trivial when compared to the day-to-day experiences of most of the world's 7.8 billion people: "Oh, woe is me! There's no decent satellite radio reception on the last mile of my commute to work! The Wi-Fi sucks at this coffee shop, and the barista didn't put enough milk in my latte! If God exists, why does He permit such suffering?"

An Elegant Headache is a lot like that—but it's even more obnoxious to complain about because it's a direct result of good fortune!

If you think clearly and rationally about almost any difficulty or setback you may have, you'll likely have an epiphany: "Wow, this problem only exists on a really high level, and I'm kind of lucky that I get to deal with it." If all of a sudden your business turns a profit, you may have tax implications that you've never dealt with before, and you could look at that as a problem. Or you could accept it as the price you pay for being successful . . . and maybe even see at it as an opportunity.

You could say, "Hey, this is awesome! I have this potential tax situation because I am profitable, and so what I'm going to do is put some of that cash back into the business, since reinvesting in the growth of my business is tax-deductible. I'm going to pay bonuses to reward the team for making these profits possible, and to foster loyalty. I'm going to invest in some long-overdue IT upgrades and a new marketing campaign. And yes, I'll still have some taxes to pay, but I'm starting the year with a little more cash than I usually do. I'm not starting at zero." There is a price to be paid for that, but it's a good investment.

Before I learned to delegate certain tasks and responsibilities, I often used to have to sit in project development meetings for two or three hours. Sometimes I still have to do that. I don't do it as much anymore as I used to—it's not what I like to do, and I'm not good at it—but for various reasons I occasionally need to be there. And after an hour or two of this tedium, in a situation not of my making or choosing, my head sometimes starts to hurt a little bit. *That's* a headache.

By way of contrast—on my honeymoon, my wife and I locked ourselves in our beautiful Mexican Riviera hotel room for twenty-four hours straight, and at the end of it, I was black and blue and dehydrated and had a terrible, pounding headache. But I would never complain about that headache. *That* was an Elegant Headache.

As a leader, you need to cultivate a foundation of gratitude. You will never have more in your life until you are grateful for what you have now, because if you haven't learned gratitude at this level, you will not learn it at a higher level. This principle is immutable.

So now is the time to practice gratitude, to be grateful for the things you have, and for the people in your life. To achieve peace and happiness, you have got to be able to mine your life for it and articulate your gratitude on a regular basis—and communicate it to the people you are grateful for.

Generosity is tremendously important for a leader. Be generous with your compliments. Be generous with your money when you have it . . . and when you don't have it, find a way to be able to give away 10 percent of what you *do* have on a regular basis. That means every time you get something, you give 10 percent of it away. It doesn't make any sense, but when you do that, you will have more of it. I've done it for the last twenty-six years, and I can't believe how well it works. When you give money away to the right causes, the right charities . . . there will always be more.

Business is like a meal: you've got all the right ingredients, but how you put them together Back Stage and how you serve them up onstage is the difference between basic sustenance and a distinctive experience for your clients, your customers, and all your other stakeholders. And we'll discuss how to do that in the next chapter.

CHAPTER 9

APPLYING THESE IDEAS
TO YOUR ENTERPRISE

@gapingvoid

THESE "POCKETS OF FREEDOM" INSIDE LARGE ORGS CREATE REALLY INTERESTING NEW VALUE. So it's your job as an entrepreneur and a leader to create as many of these pockets for other people as possible.

- Hugh MacLeod

LIVING THE MODEL

One of the things I learned during the Great Recession is that we don't ask for tough times in our lives. Just ask anyone: nobody will tell you, "I can't wait till that really tough time comes." But every entrepreneur would probably say that they learned more during the tough times than they did during the good times. Those are the times that will get your attention and get you focused.

So we got through the recession, developed this model, and started using it a little. But we weren't fully exploiting it; we still had poor processes and procedures. You can use the Q^3 Quad Mod to organize your business, but if you're not committed to putting the processes, procedures, and systems in place, and putting the right people in place, then it's just another cute idea. That's the difference between having an idea and using an idea—having the model versus *living* the model.

It's important to be able to identify where things are going right or going wrong, but you must use what you've learned to put things in place.

FIRST STEPS

Having read most of this book, by now you're likely asking yourself whether everything in it applies to your own situation, and how. You may be thinking, "But I don't have a Design Quadrant! How does this apply to *my* business?"

The first requirement of philosophy—and the first step toward implementing the Q^3 Quad Mod or any other organizational system—is to define your terms. You need to evaluate your organization—what is your Front Stage and what is your Back Stage? Which people, and which roles, fit into which quadrants? And besides people and their roles, what *other* aspects of the business fall into which quadrants?

So here's step one for you: Do an activity inventory for your business. Draw a cross on a sheet of paper and label the four quadrants separated by that cross: Marketing, Design, Production, and Operations. Then consider what each member of your team does (or what each department does, if your organization is large). Maybe you have someone whose role, at first glance, isn't easily definable in terms of these four quadrants, but she's always working to attract new business—going out there and talking to people, maintaining and updating your social media presence, and so on. That's marketing.

OK, now design. What aspect of your organization makes up the Design Quadrant? That's one a lot of people don't think they have, but in many cases what may appear to be a part of the Marketing or Production Quadrant is actually Design.

Take, for example, an auto dealer's showroom—it's the physical presentation of your image, right? But is your image an aspect of marketing . . . or design? There's the people part of it to consider—the interaction between your people and the public—but your image also does the job of attracting new business. Getting people to come to your showroom or to visit your website is marketing . . . and the website itself is design.

If you're a real estate agent, your version of marketing is finding new clients, or making sure your Facebook ads are reaching as many people as you need them to. Your version of design is staging a house, or holding an open house. Your version of production is documents—how you keep track of your sales. In another kind of business, that kind of thing might be operations, but for a real estate agent, the sales and the documents that attest to them are *what you produce* . . . so they're part of the Production Quadrant.

If you're a dentist, how is your office decorated and furnished? How is your office staff dressed, and how straight and clean are their teeth? Those are design issues. In some dental offices, the light shining on patients while getting their teeth cleaned is designed to be warmer and easier to tolerate—they don't have a fluorescent bulb in their eyes. The dentist uses numbing medication and warm water if a patient has sensitive teeth. The client experience is all part of design. Production, for a dentist, is making you a crown, or drilling a cavity. Operations is invoicing the insurance companies and following up on that to make sure they get their payments on time.

My dentist has a great Front Stage (albeit a very different one than he had before March of 2020!). First of all, he's very personable. He knows enough about you to ask a few good questions that make you think he really *gets* who you are. I'm sure he has a CRM that he reviews Back Stage: "OK, Jeff's a pilot; he owns his own business; he employs about thirty people; he is married to Melanie, who is a coach, and he has four kids." Knowing those details and having them fresh in his mind when I sit down in his chair enables him to have a nice two- to five-minute conversation with me, and makes me feel like we're really connected and he actually cares about me.

So his activity on the Back Stage is to have his team collect a couple of pieces of information about who you are, either from a questionnaire you fill out when you first come in or from conversations that the hygienist has with you. His team then puts that information in your file so that anybody who works on your teeth from that point forward knows who you are. They know you like mint-flavored polishing compound, or that you're terrified of the Novocain needle. The practical effect of all this Back Stage activity—which is invisible to me, so I'm only guessing at the particulars—is that when I'm sitting in his chair, I feel like a rock star.

But isn't everybody who works in a dentist's office on the Front Stage? After all, every single person working there has important direct contact with patients. In different ways and to different degrees, everybody in a dentist's office has both Front Stage and Back Stage responsibilities: the receptionist who greets you may also handle appointment scheduling and other operations tasks. The dentist himself, after the office closes for the night, goes home and has a quick dinner and then probably spends a couple of hours in his home office going over financials.

Even in companies for which this is true, that overlap between the Front and Back Stages doesn't mean there is no distinction to be made between the two. There is very definitely a Back Stage at the dentist's office—and for my dentist, it comprises those horrible-looking tools and implements and suction things that frighten adults almost as much as they frighten children. The smart businesses that have a highly technical Back Stage will maintain an air of mystery about it. I don't want to see all those tools and implements—or any part of the grungy side of his practice—and he knows that, so he keeps it well hidden until some piece needs to be brought out and used . . . which is usually after I'm already laid out in the chair staring at the ceiling and won't notice.

So yes, the dentist's office is almost all Front Stage, but a lot of Back Stage pieces have to be brought to the Front Stage from time to time, and so you need to really think about your process—how you deliver that service and still maintain that high level of glamour. My dentist is a healthcare professional, not a marketing or design specialist . . . but the image part of what he does is flawless.

Once you have some semblance of a working picture of how the Q^3 Quad Mod maps onto your own organizational structure (or at least, how you would like it to), then ask your-self—or ask a trusted and capable member of your management team—which people need to have better relationships with others who are working in the same quadrant? Or in different quadrants?

TRUST YOUR INTUITION

Let's talk about intuition within the context of how to apply these ideas. You might not know everything that needs to happen in all quadrants at all times, but if you are going to be an effective entrepreneur, you must have *intuition*. You need some sense of what you are doing and what needs to be done.

This is more than just the "time and place" conversation. This has to do with how the various parts of your organization all work together, and then how that enterprise gets bundled—Front Stage, Back Stage, and all four quadrants—and presented to the world.

If you're just starting out as an entrepreneur, I want to try to clear the clouds away from the mountain so that you can see the importance of working on your intuitiveness. You may have knowledge and experience, but these, by themselves, are not the complete toolbox you need to be an entrepreneur. In addition to knowledge, you need to have wisdom. Wisdom is the correct application of knowledge, and the correct application of knowledge requires intuition.

You gain intuition through experience: your power of intuition when you first start your organization is going to be very different from the level of intuition you'll have after you've spent ten years running that organization. But while you are gaining experience, and as you are starting your company, I urge you to expand your thinking to include this in the list of ingredients that you want to throw into the stew that is your business. I want to make entrepreneurs aware of the fact that intuition is very important—and very different from feelings.

One of the biggest obstacles young entrepreneurs face is what I call the "prove it" mindset. When I was young I was very much a *prove it* guy. I've always been a quick start; I've always been willing to just dive into things. But when it came down to the nuts and bolts of a situation, I wanted to know the size of the nuts and bolts. And how many nuts do we have, versus how many bolts? I was too concerned with nailing down details to trust my intuition. *Prove it,* I always said.

I think that's the domain of young people in general, and perhaps young entrepreneurs in particular, and a little bit of that is not a bad thing. Plenty of struggling entrepreneurs are loaded with vision but don't have any grip on day-to-day, concrete reality. That's not a good thing . . . but neither is it good to always be insisting, "*Prove it, prove it, prove it, prove it.* I'm not going to believe it until I see it." Approaching things that way hinders your ability to make decisions and slows down all your processes—and that's the gap that intuition fills.

After learning this principle, it took me fifteen years to begin to apply it. One of my business coaches said to me, "You know that feeling you get inside when you are in a situation that doesn't seem right? That visceral, gut reaction? You need to trust that, because it will rarely let you down." It took me fifteen years to learn to trust my intuition, but when I did, I found myself walking away from opportunities because they did not seem right. I don't want to say "feel" right, because it wasn't a feeling—it was an intuition, based on years of seeing how people react, sensing motivations, and noticing that psychic peripheral vision we all have. That intuition might be based on the chemistry between me and the person I'm dealing with, or it might be the type of project and how it is funded, or any of a myriad of different things. I may not notice these things consciously at first, but my intuition will pick up on them; I just need to be perceptive enough to notice.

There's one situation in particular that stands out in my mind. We sat down with this client and had a wonderful meeting . . . but the guy was the devil. Satan is smooth as silk, and this guy was even smoother. He was engaging and charming, but the project had trouble written all over it. I don't think he was trying to deceive us—it was maybe just excessive optimism on his part—but after I asked the developer a few questions, the truth finally came out: "Yes, that person you met with is in a very strong position to be able to sue you." And that had been my biggest concern. We backed out of that project, and, sure enough, I don't think it went really well for anybody who was ultimately involved in it.

PURSUE RELATIONSHIPS; DON'T CHASE PROJECTS

We were interested in that job because it was a prestige project . . . but a good entrepreneur will try not to chase projects for their own sake.

That's why we don't do design competitions—because we'd be chasing a project. You do a whole bunch of work, you don't get paid for it, it's bureaucratic, it's political, and there's a whole lot of backroom stuff that you have no influence on. You can't use any of your relationship skills; they just pick a "winner."

When you chase projects, you look at a great piece of property, and it's a great site, and it's going to be a high-profile project—a landmark building in a prominent location, like a civic center or a town hall or a public library. Those kinds of projects look great in your portfolio, and completing one is a feather in your cap. When you sit down with prospective clients you can tell them, "I designed the civic center," and they go, "Oh my gosh, that building is a masterpiece. I can't believe you got it done! Oh man, that's wonderful. You guys must really know what you're doing."

All business professionals have their version of chasing a project: they chase an idea, and it doesn't go well. Don't do that. What you want to do instead, as an entrepreneur, is cultivate relationships. People don't do business with projects; people do business with relationships. And that doesn't apply just to creative fields like architecture. Even if you are manufacturing and selling widgets, you have to have relationships with distribution people, retailers, etc., and your path to success lies in building those relationships, because they are going to take you to places that just price and product will not.

The other side of the coin would be a situation in which you are desperate for business. You need revenue, so you may find you're willing to compromise some of your values in terms of who you're willing to work with—because you need the work. Those are two compromises that you would make for two very different reasons, but they both lead to trouble.

FOCUS!

You have choices to make on a daily basis: "We need a little bit more here and a little bit less over there. This quadrant needs a little bolstering, so we need to focus on it a little more." The best thing you can do as a leader, relative to the four quadrants, is the one thing that most leaders have trouble doing: keep your focus. Ask yourself, "What are we trying to do here?"

When I learned to ask that question, it transformed my business. "What are we trying to do here? What is really going on and why? Is this serving our business, is this helping us to succeed as an organization . . . or am I doing it because it's busywork that makes me feel good?" I ask myself those questions about every interaction that happens in all the quadrants, because if you don't stop to do that—to refocus—you can get so far into the weeds that you become lost and forget where you were even trying to get in the first place. *Whoa, wait a minute, what are we trying to do here?*

I can be my own worst enemy. "Should this report ideally look like this—or like *this*? This building . . . we could add this and this and this and this . . . "

Our design principal grounds me at times like this. "Yeah," he'll say, "we could do that, but it changes the style, and it's not what the client wants."

The freedom that you have as an entrepreneur can be intoxicating. When you're first starting out, it's like, "*Woo-hoo!* I can do what I want now!" But you need to be restrained and say to yourself, "That's too much. There's no value there. I'm just doing it to make me feel good."

Intuition and inspiration have a flip side, and you need to temper them. You can say, "I've got all these ideas!" and be involved in every single minute thing that happens in the business, but if you do that, you're going to burn yourself out, and you are not going to be happy.

The primary goal of any business is to stay in business. And when an entrepreneur gets too enamored with an idea, a product, or a market, or with notoriety, he or she can lose focus, and then that Q^3 Quad Mod can no longer stay balanced. An entrepreneur can take down the entire organization by a lack of restraint, a lack of intuition, or a lack of objectivity about what the organization really needs to do on any given day.

CONCLUSION—IT'S ABOUT FREEDOM

I recently spoke to an independent contractor, a friend who does hair and makeup and nails and whatever else women get—hair extensions, eyelashes, etc. I said, "I'm almost done with my second book."

She asked, "What's it about?"

"It's about structure," I said. "It's a model for how to structure your business. A lot of people start businesses because they are really good at one thing, but there are other components that go into a business that they don't do very well."

"What do you mean?"

I said, "There's the Front Stage, which is what you do and how you interact with people, and there's the Back Stage—how you bill, how you pay your expenses, et cetera."

"Oh my gosh," she said, "that is such a mess. I hate that part of my business, I don't do it well."

So I asked her, "Do you know somebody who is a bookkeeper?" And she said, "Well, yeah, one of my clients is a bookkeeper."

I told her the client could probably spend two hours a week and get her books completely done. "All your billing, all your compliance—everything. How would you feel then?"

Her eyes lit up with excitement. "Oh my gosh, that's . . . that's brilliant. Because I just want to do what I do."

And that brings us back to the concept of *entrepreneurial freedom* that we discussed in Chapter 1. She just wants to do what she does—and you just want to do what you do, without getting bogged down in the stuff you *don't* do that nonetheless needs to get done.

I'm trying to help entrepreneurs understand that they may ultimately employ people within the different quadrants to do this stuff, but just being a small business doesn't mean that you don't have other resources available to you. My friend with the salon was frustrated and overwhelmed, and that's why she talked to me about it. She saw all the aspects of her business that didn't involve working on her clients' hair and nails as a big, amorphous set of complex problems with no definition.

This amorphous thing is like a couple of drops of oil on a concrete floor: it looks like there is a tremendous amount of oil, even though there's less than an ounce. But if you get a squeegee and a paper towel and you pull it together and give it some shape, you realize it really wasn't that much oil. When you put a few boundaries on the amorphous mess that you *think* you have, you realize that you really don't have that much of a mess.

And that's what I am trying to help people understand: a structure appears when you begin to look at the separate components of your business, and then you can begin to identify what it is that you hate to do—and find someone who can do it better than you can.

This brings us back to the activity inventory that I talked about in Chapter 8. When you begin to list all the things you do, you'll find there's maybe a dozen of them that you shouldn't be doing. I should not be going on social media looking at what my competition is doing. It doesn't serve me well, it's a waste of time, and I have no use for that information once I get it. That's one activity I can take off my list. In your case, there may be other activities to eliminate or reassign, or other people besides you who need to be assigned to different tasks. Maybe you run an auto repair shop, and your mechanic does the inspections. He's really good at it . . . but he's not *great* at it. What he *is* great at is calling up potential clients and saying, "Hey, I've got a spot in my schedule for you next week, would you like to come in?" And people love him because they know he's really good at what he does. He has credibility, and that's what he should be doing, rather than turning wrenches.

As for you, you may love turning wrenches . . . but you didn't become an entrepreneur so you could turn wrenches. You became an entrepreneur so you could lead an organization. If you don't want to lead the organization, then you have to relinquish that responsibility to someone who will. That's a much tougher model to get to, but it is obtainable.

But until you assess what categories the various activities of your organization fall into, you're not going to know how amorphous and undefined your organization is. So the first tool to use is the activity inventory that you laid out: eliminate activities that don't answer the question, "Why are we doing this?"

Next, determine which things fall into the Front Stage and the Back Stage: "OK, now which of these activities are marketing? Well, what *is* marketing? Marketing is how I attract and bring in new business. OK, what falls into that category? What do I do well (and love to do), what do I not do well (or not love to do)? Who else could do this? What resources are available, either within my organization or outside of it?"

Same thing with design. Design is your image (of which marketing is part), but packaged in a certain way that communicates the value it represents to your audience.

The magic is actually not in the hemispheres—Front Stage and Back Stage. The magic is in the flow that exists within them and between them. And when you determine which activities belong in which boxes, and everyone is able to focus on which of those they themselves should be doing, you can harness that magic to benefit your organization more than you may be able to imagine.

CHAPTER 10

SHOULD WE CONTINUE THE CONVERSATION?

THE REAL VALUE OF A COMPANY IS CREATED IN THE COLLABORATIONS BETWEEN PEOPLE, NOT BY THE JOB DESCRIPTIONS THEY OCCUPY. Yet your standard org chart makes no mention of this. This might need to change.

- Hugh MacLeod

THE NEXT STEP

I met with four people in my office yesterday, and they each gave me about three minutes' worth of information about their businesses and their lives. That took a total of fifteen minutes, and then I spent the next thirty minutes telling them all the things they needed to be working on and where I saw shortcomings in their businesses and their business plans. They hugged me and thanked me profusely. They are my friends for life. They think I'm a genius because I nailed down what they do and what they *need* to do.

And I love doing that. They had the right heart. They gave me permission to be completely upfront and transparent and honest with my sense of who they were and what they were going through.

I was working alone that day, without Chelsea, but when Chelsea and I work with people together, it gets a lot richer and a lot deeper and there are a lot more takeaways.

We would love to be able to do that for you.

Please understand, we're not doing this to stay in business; we're doing just fine with our architecture practice. We're doing this because we love it and because we know it's a tremendous benefit to people and, frankly, because we can't help ourselves. As it says in the Bible, "let those that have ears hear."

I would say that 90 percent of all the people in business whom I've explained this model to have fallen in love with it.

I'd like to tell you a story that has to do with intuition and knowledge, and the correct application of knowledge—wisdom—which requires tremendous intuition.

Henry Ford once had a problem: his production line was shut down because one of the machines wasn't working properly. So he brought in an expert, and the expert looked at the production line. He looked at one of the machines. He thought for several minutes. He took out a piece of chalk. He drew a white X on the floor. He said, "Move that machine to this spot and you will be fine."

Ford called him back a couple of days later and said, "It worked! You're a genius. Send me a bill."

So the consultant sent Ford a bill, and Ford was aghast. He called the guy back and said, "You were in my plant for an hour, and you charged me $10,000 for a white X! Can you please itemize the bill?"

So the consultant sent Mr. Ford back a new invoice, which read:

One white chalk X—$1
Knowing where to put the white X—$9,999

Value and time are not related. Attorneys are notorious for billing hours for outrageous minutiae, aren't they? Well, if you're in a business that bills hourly, you have to do the kinds of things that attorneys do—say, driving to a meeting at a client's office, for which they get paid for travel time. Everyone agrees that that's fair . . . but then they may be tempted to call you on the way and have a half-hour conversation with you on the drive—for which they bill you. So now they've billed you for driving out to see you as well as for that half an hour they spent talking to you about your case while driving: they've figured out how to multiply time!

That's the only place you can be creative when you bill hourly.

Chelsea and I or any of the other professional designers who work with us can walk onto a site can look at what needs to be done, and in an hour, they can crank out a plan that nails it for the client. *Nails it*—and the client is thrilled with it. If we got paid by the time that it took to do that, we wouldn't be very successful. But we tell people that we get paid for the value that we bring, and how long it takes is an integral part of our secret sauce, our eleven herbs and spices, the magic behind the curtain . . . it's Back Stage. Our ability to do that is the byproduct of years of training, experience, mistakes, investment in the dumb tax, and, ultimately, the correct application of intuition and wisdom. If it takes one hour or twenty, we will do whatever is needed to make you happy.

Now, we're gambling that we can get it done in less than twenty hours, which is what we have budgeted for it, but if it is the right solution for you, you shouldn't care how long it took. I don't care how long it took my dentist to make that new crown for me. I just care that it came out well and I look good.

That's value-added service. That's what we do. We love to help people find ways to bring the value out in their business.

That's the value of having us work with you for half a day. It's about taking knowledge and wisdom and intuition and bringing them together in a package that gets you results quickly with just a few tools and a willingness to be objective and honest about where you are and where you want to go.

We're the white chalk X, and that's why you should work with us. We're going to charge you handsomely, but in return you are going to achieve a profound understanding of what your value proposition is and what's going on in your organization—and these things will happen in a very short amount of time because our work is tremendously focused.

Not everyone needs us; for some the book will be enough. Some people are going to read this and go, "Ahh, I get it! It's a lightning bolt! I've got clarity!" And they are going to be able to apply everything. But for the people who do need us . . . sometimes it's easier for an outsider to see into your business or into your life than it is for you to self-evaluate. And sometimes you know you could do it yourself, but it'll take you a year because you'll have a hard time allocating time and focus to it.

All progress starts by telling the truth. If you are doing really well, you are satisfied with where you are, and I've given you a few tools to help refine how your business works, then great! But if you're in a situation where you're kind of stuck, we'd love to help you out. If the relationship seems right, if you talk to us and we seem like we're a fit for your organization from a cultural standpoint, and you'd benefit from what we can do, we'd be glad to spend a day or two with you to help you figure out how you can take things to the next level and get unstuck.

I want people to know that I am passionate about this model. It's why I created the model, and it's why we wrote this book. I believe it will change your business and your life—but you have to want it. We're not trying to convince people to work with us; we're doing just fine with our architecture firm. This is really about you.

Could your organization be a lot better?

ENDNOTES

Chapter 1: You Can't Have Entrepreneurial Freedom with Yesterday's Org Chart

1   Pofeldt, Elaine. "New Data: More Americans Are Creating Million-Dollar, One-Person Businesses." Forbes. Forbes Magazine, May 29, 2017. https://www.forbes.com/sites/elainepofeldt/2017/05/25/new-data-more-americans-are-creating-million-dollar-one-person-businesses/?sh=4fecbd996239.

2   Sullivan, Dan. "The 4 Freedoms That Motivate Successful Entrepreneurs." Strategic Coach. Accessed January 8, 2021. https://resources.strategiccoach.com/the-multiplier-mindset-blog/the-4-freedoms-that-motivate-successful-entrepreneurs.

Chapter 4: The Marketing Quadrant

1   Welch, William M., Jon Swartz, and Gary Strauss. "Two Dead, 168 Hurt in San Francisco Air Crash." USA Today. Gannett Satellite Information Network, July 7, 2013. https://www.usatoday.com/story/travel/news/2013/07/06/airline-crash-san-francisco/2495099/.

2   Lencioni, Patrick. Death by Meeting: a Leadership Fable about Solving the Most Painful Problem in Business. San Francisco: Jossey-Bass A Wiley Imprint, 2004.

Chapter 6: The Production Quadrant

1   RLane, Randall. "Bezos Unbound: Exclusive Interview With The Amazon Founder On What He Plans To Conquer Next." Forbes. Forbes Magazine, February 21, 2019. https://www.forbes.com/sites/randalllane/2018/08/30/bezos-unbound-exclusive-interview-with-the-amazon-founder-on-what-he-plans-to-conquer-next/?sh=5f5ba265647b.

Chapter 8: Lightning Bolt Leadership: In Charge, Not in Control

1   Sullivan, Dan. "What Is The Ceiling Of Complexity?" Resources, n.d. https://resources.strategiccoach.com/the-multiplier-mindset-blog/what-is-the-ceiling-of-complexity.

ABOUT THE AUTHOR

Jeffrey DeMure, AIA, is a visionary architect with over 35 years in professional practice, and the founder of Jeffrey DeMure + Associates Architects Planners, Inc. (JD+A) Jeffrey and his talented team trademarked Livable Design™, a revolutionary collection of simple, cost-effective elements that make any living space fully inclusive for residents and guests of all ages and mobility profiles. In 2018, Jeff published his first book *Livable Design: From Commodity to Community with Affordable, Adaptable, Beautiful Home Design.*

An in-demand nationally recognized speaker (forums include PCBC, ULI, NAHB's International Builders Show, The Seaside Institute, and LeadingAge), Jeff also serves on numerous boards and advisory committees with the goal of sharing his vision for the future of the industry—a world where our homes and communities are built to grow with us over the course of an entire lifetime. As a designer and a creative insti-gator, Jeff is leading the conversation on crafting spaces with intention. His philosophy is that simple, efficient, and beautiful spaces lead to better living.

Since founding JD+A in 2004, Jeff has evolved his talents to designing and crafting a successful entrepreneurial business. He designed a simple and profound model for organizing and analyzing entrepreneurial organizations, the Q^3 Quad Mod, which is the subject of his second book, *Death to the Org Chart*. He works with entrepreneurs and industry leaders to help them evaluate, rebalance, and restructure their businesses using this model with spectacular success. Jeff is also an active leader in his church, a commercial pilot, and devoted husband to Melanie, with whom he has four beautiful children, Emily, JT, Jeremy, and Brayden.